M000308652

Re-create Your Life

To try the belief process described in
this book for free, please go to
www.RecreateYourLife.com

Re-create Your Life

Transforming Yourself and Your World with The Lefkoe Method®

Morty Lefkoe

DMI Publishing
A division of The Lefkoe Institute® LLC
Novato, California

Re-create Your Life: Transforming Yourself and
Your World with The Lefkoe Method®

copyright © 1997 by Morty Lefkoe.
All rights reserved. Printed in U.S.A. No part of this book may be used or reproduced in any manner whatsoever without written permission except in the case of reprints in the context of reviews. For information, write DMI Publishing, a division of The Lefkoe Institute LLC, 760 Arlington Circle, Novato, CA 94947.
www.mortylefkoe.com

Library of Congress Cataloging-in-Publication Data
Lefkoe, Morty
Re-create your life: transforming yourself and your world with Lefkoe Method® / by Morty Lefkoe.
p.   cm.
Includes bibliographical references (p.) and index.
ISBN 978-0615782386 (PAPERBACK)
1. Decision-making.   2. Problem solving.   3. Thought and thinking.
4. Change (Psychology)   I. Title.
BF448.L44   1997
153.8'3—dc20   96-43406
                                                  CIP

Lyrics from "Pick Yourself Up" used by permission. Written by Dorothy Fields and Jerome Kern, copyright © 1936 PolyGram International Publishing, Inc. (and as designated by co-publisher). Copyright renewed. All rights reserved.

Excerpt from "Nuclear Language and How We Learned to Pat the Bomb" by Carol Cohn, as appeared in SIGNS: *The Journal of Women in Culture and Society* used by permission. Copyright © 1987 The University of Chicago.

Author's note: Many of the names and identifying circumstances of the people in this book have been changed to protect individuals' privacy.

To Shelly

my best friend, partner, and wife.
Thank you for the difference you make in my life daily.

To Blake and Brittany

the two girls who have given me
my proudest title: Daddy.
Thank you for your daily lessons on life and for your love.

Contents

Acknowledgments

*O*ver *thirteen thousand private clients*—thanks for your trust and for allowing me and the other Lefkoe Method® facilitators to work with you, because without you there wouldn't be a Lefkoe Method®. What I've learned about it since I initially created it has been through our work with you.

My many friends, Jane O'Leary, Jeanne and Dan Fauci, David Ferber, Sherrylee and Sam Mink, Ruth Bonomo. Arlene Lefkoe, Lynda and Stuart Brodsky, Diz and Sam Gutner, Margaret Hiatt, Jamie and Glenn Forbes, Joyce Cohen, Lucie and Mark Scanlon, Elissa and Bryan Russo, David and Debbie Howland-Murray (who designed a brilliant logo for The Lefkoe Method® Institute), Marcia Bandes, Tom Edwards, and many others too numerous to mention by name—thanks for your support over the years, both financial and moral. I especially thank those of you who read early versions of this book and gave me valuable feedback.

Dr. Larry Dossey, a modern-day Renaissance man and friend—thanks for being the first person to help me realize that I could never present the full scope of The Lefkoe Method® Technology in articles and for repeatedly encouraging me to introduce my ideas in a book.

Elizabeth Campbell, a teacher at the California Institute for Integral Studies where I was registered in a Ph.D. program a few years ago—thanks for urging me to turn the paper describing The Lefkoe Method® that I submitted to you as an assignment into a book and for your excellent suggestions as you read the early chapters.

Ron Bandes—thanks for preparing a videotape that vividly communicated the exciting results of my prison research and for your many insightful comments as you read the innumerable drafts of this book.

Sarah Engel—thanks for suggesting a way to revise the structure of my book so readers would realize from the beginning that I was presenting a revolutionary technology for change in every area of life rather than a self-help technique useful only for individuals.

All my associates at Lefkoe & Associates, Inc., the predecessor company to The Lefkoe Method® Institute—thanks for helping me to discover and implement the first application of The Lefkoe Method® to organizations.

Werner Erhard—thanks for my first exposure to transformation, for assisting me to shift my life from a focus on "what's in it for me" to a focus on contributing to others, and for the immeasurable difference you have made in the lives of hundreds of thousands of people through the est training and the Hunger Project.

Hilda and Jack Fogel, the best in-laws a man could have—thanks for welcoming me into your family, for treating me like your son, and for your constant love and confidence in me. I especially want to acknowledge you, Mom, for using The Lefkoe Method to demonstrate that it is never too late—even when you are in your seventies—to transform your life. I love you both very much.

Letha Edwards, the first person other than my wife who was trained as a Lefkoe Method® facilitator—thanks for being my partner and second-best friend and for your unwavering love and support.

Chris Schillig, my editor—thanks for your initial enthusiasm about the ideas I wanted to express, for telling me what was good and what wasn't so good about my manuscript, and for advising me what was needed for it to reach the widest possible audience.

Catherine Whitney—thanks for doing a magnificent job in helping me translate some complex ideas into readable prose. You helped me transform a manuscript that read like a textbook into a page turner.

Cynthia Borg, Director of Publicity and Promotion at Andrews and McMeel—thanks for support "above and beyond" and for being my "advocate."

Mauna Eichner, who designed the book cover and jacket—thanks for capturing the essence of my message in a highly imaginative and unique visual image.

Janet Baker—thanks for a truly amazing job of copyediting.

Jane Dystel and Charles Myer, my agents—thanks for believing in me, my vision, and my manuscript after other agents had turned me down, for finding the right publisher, and for teaching me what I needed to know about the publishing business.

Blake and Brittany, my two daughters—thanks for the joy you bring to my life, for being the reason I feel so much love every day that it hurts, for being understanding about the time that Mommy and I are in "sessions," and for being the incredible human beings you have created yourselves to be. I am so proud of you I could burst.

Shelly, my wife, best friend, soul mate, and partner—thanks for loving and supporting me, for enduring all the hard times, and for your confidence in me and my vision. You contribute to the life of everyone who is fortunate enough to meet you, especially the parents who attend your workshops. I never could have done what I did or become what I am without you. You have made a profound difference in my life. I love you.

Re-create Your Life

Prologue

My Personal Journey

The significant problems we have cannot be solved at the same level of thinking we were at when we created them.

—Albert Einstein

Before the age of thirty-eight, my main interest in life was making lots of money and becoming a famous business executive. Success for me would have been having several million dollars in the bank and my picture on the cover of _Fortune_ magazine. This goal led me to become a management consultant and writer. As a consultant I helped organizations develop effective communications and marketing programs. I also wrote more than a hundred freelance articles about business and government for publications like _Fortune_, the _Wall Street Journal_, _Nation's Business_, and _Barron's_.

I was very logical and rational and was generally out of touch with my feelings. I would have described myself as very practical and not at all spiritual.

I was driven in my work and motivated by my goals for success. But deep down I was confused and unhappy. As the years went by, I found that I was depressed much of the time. Eventually, I tried both private and group psychotherapy, which helped me to cope better with my day-to-day existence. However, neither was able to eliminate the negative sense I had about myself and my life.

2

The Start of My Transformation

At the age of thirty-eight I took the est training and experienced an immediate and fundamental shift in my life. I was no longer obsessed with impressing others and achieving wealth and fame. My commitment shifted to contributing to others.[1]

Shortly after I completed the est training in New York City in 1975, the organization offered me a job in San Francisco, where I managed the Public Information Office and handled many special projects. After two and a half years, I left and moved back to New York, where I continued to assist at est, leading almost twenty different seminars for three thousand or so est graduates and assisting in about twenty trainings.

My last project at est was helping Werner Erhard create the Hunger Project (THP), which is devoted to ending world hunger. I assisted in the production of the original events that introduced THP to about 35,000 people. Later, I worked with Werner in writing the *Source Document* that spelled out the principles of THP and what it would take to eliminate death by starvation on the planet. This was my first attempt to think systematically about how to use ideas to make radical global change. More and more, I was seeing that such change was possible—something I never would have imagined a few years earlier. I was exhilarated by the idea that I could contribute to that change.

After leaving est I returned to consulting, but it was not at all satisfying. I was no longer the same person I had been before my est experience. I had begun a personal path to understand myself, to become more "spiritual," and to find some way of making a real difference in organizations and in the world. I could no longer get excited about giving companies advice on how to communicate or market more effectively.

I was also frustrated by the results of my conventional consulting methods. I noticed with increasing frequency that organizations, having retained me and agreed with my suggestions, often failed to follow through. I checked with a number of other consulting firms, small and large, and all of them agreed that unless they held the client's hand and walked them through a specific recommendation, it usually wasn't implemented. This baffled me. Why would an organization pay to get advice, agree with the advice, and then do nothing?

As I pondered this curious situation, I realized that this inability to do what made good sense was also true for individuals, not just organizations. How often did people read a book or get advice to do something and decide to pursue it (like exercising more or dieting), but then never get around to doing it? Conversely, how often did people get involved in activities or relationships they knew were wrong for them?

Why Do We Do What We Do?

I set out on an intellectual quest to understand the source of individual and organizational behavior. I read extensively on subjects ranging from the nature of human consciousness to organizational transformation to leading-edge science. I took many workshops. In time, I concluded that what people did, felt, and experienced was determined by their *beliefs*: about themselves, other people, and life itself—a realization that many others, including Buddhists, have had for centuries. I came to understand why people and organizations did what they did and why it was hard for them to change their behavior—even when they wanted to—*if they hadn't first changed their beliefs*. But knowing that beliefs were at the core of individual and organizational behavior was only the first step. I still had to discover how to *change* those beliefs.

Finding the solution became my sole focus. I began my search by totally altering the nature of my consulting practice. Instead of giving organizations advice on how to solve problems, which they frequently didn't use anyway, I started to consider what it would take to assist organizations to solve their own problems by helping them change their beliefs.

Around that time, a friend of mine, Terry Shull, who had worked at AT&T, suggested that we create a workshop for service technicians employed by local companies that had just split off from AT&T. If we could find a way to help service technicians provide the higher level of service that customers were demanding, Terry said, we ought to get a lot of business. It was clear that the conventional approach of merely telling service technicians what to do, how to do it, and why to do it would not produce the dramatic improvement that was needed. On the other hand, if we could shift the way they defined their job—from being "service technicians" to being "customer satisfiers"—so they really believed their essential purpose was to make customers happy, a dramatic increase in the level of service was possible. I created a workshop designed to help people experience their jobs differently and then set out to market it. For almost a year I called, wrote, and met with many companies. I kept getting expressions of interest but no sales. During that period I was also consumed by another question: What would it take to change beliefs *permanently*? I continued to read and do a lot of thinking.

While I was trying to market my new workshop, I had stopped marketing my "advice-giving" consulting services. After six months, I was in desperate financial straits. But I didn't want to go back to giving advice to organizations, because it had become clear to me that the advice, good though it might be, made little difference to the client.

In January 1985, I had the opportunity to make a presentation in California to Carter Hawley Hale (CHH), the department store chain. The state of California had offered the company a grant of several million dollars to take 1,500 people who were on unemployment or welfare and train them in the retail profession. The state's theory was that if these people could get job skills and the guarantee of a job for at least six months, they would become productive tax-paying citizens and require less state aid in the long run than the amount of the training grant.

I had heard about this project from a friend, who said that CHH had already created a six-week training program: three weeks in a classroom and three in a store. But the company was concerned that the trainees might have a motivation problem, so they wanted to spend a couple of days on motivation at the start of the workshop.

This seemed like an ideal opportunity for me. I made a call to one of the Human Resource people at CHH and told her about my work. I explained what I had learned about the nature of motivation.

"You want to motivate these trainees," I said. "That's easy. The difficulty is that motivation is a feeling that lasts only a day, a week, or a month, and then it's gone. A more effective method," I suggested, "would be to help the trainees discover and eliminate any beliefs that might get in the way of their success in the program."

I told her I could create a workshop that would accomplish that, and she invited me out to California to discuss my proposal. I wasn't sure exactly how to go about it, but, as was my want, I thought if I got the assignment I would figure out how to do what I had promised.

My Trip to California

On January 2, I was on a plane from New York to Los Angeles with five hours on my hands, and I found myself thinking about my own life. I had been struggling for a long time to get companies to accept my programs. But in spite of making many presentations, I wasn't getting clients. Here I was again, flying cross-country to try once more. I thought of the old Fred Astaire song from the movie *Swing Time*: "Pick yourself up, dust yourself off, and start all over again." That was my pattern, repeated day after day. Well, I wondered, if my life was the result of my beliefs, what did I believe that could be responsible for the pattern I had just identified in my life?

I had always seen myself as someone who never gave up. No matter what, I'd keep going. In fact, that was the one trait most people who knew me always acknowledged. So what did I actually believe? Five hundred or so miles later I had found the answer: **I'm someone who overcomes obstacles**. That was the truth about me. In fact, it felt as if that's who I really was.

If one's life is a function of one's beliefs, I thought, what would show up in my life if I believed **I'm someone who overcomes obstacles**?

Obstacles, of course! Not success, because that wouldn't give me an opportunity to demonstrate that I'd never give up. I needed obstacles to prove that nothing could ever stop me. And I had been proving it all my life, especially during the past year or so.

I continued to question. Where did I get that idea from? Why did I think that? I thought and wrote for almost five hours. By the time I landed I felt different, as if something profound had shifted in me, but I didn't know what.

After I made my presentation at CHH, they told me they were interviewing one more consultant and would get back to me in ten days. I returned home the next day still musing over the remarkable shift I had experienced on the plane. What had happened to me? What did it mean?

I had just started trying to explain to my wife, Shelly, what had happened to me when the phone rang. It was CHH. I had gotten the assignment. They had liked my presentation so much that they decided not to even interview the other consultant. CHH wanted me to create a three-day workshop that would assist the trainees to eliminate any belief that might inhibit their ability to be successful sales associates. My course would be used at the start of the six-week program. Because there were to be so many groups, however, I wouldn't be able to lead my own workshop. I would have to create it and then teach the company's trainers how to lead it.

I hung up the phone and turned back to my wife. "It looks like I really did eliminate a belief, because the obstacles just disappeared. I got the assignment!"

Shelly was thrilled. "Tell me what you did on the plane," she pleaded.

"I'm not sure," I answered honestly. I had to find out what I had done to make the belief go away because not only didn't I have the belief anymore, something had changed in my life. I was certain this shift in me was the key to what I was looking for in my work. If I could help people have the same kind of transformational experience, my work with organizations would have unlimited possibilities.

The Lefkoe Method

Eventually I was able to write down the steps to what I came to call The Lefkoe Method (TLM) Process. I had created a technique that would assist individuals to identify the specific beliefs that determined their behavior, feelings, and attitudes and then to totally eliminate those beliefs. Although TLM has been modified and improved since its creation, the basic principles are still the same. Initially, I didn't "figure out" TLM. I didn't use a process of deduction to arrive at the steps. Rather, I intuitively did something that worked, after which I did a lot of hard thinking to figure out how and why it worked and how to improve it.

I immediately found ways to apply TLM to the field of organizational transformation. Instead of giving companies advice on what to do, I now had a method to help them change their "cultures" (their beliefs about what it took to survive and succeed), as well as the beliefs of individual workers. Using TLM, companies could determine on their own what needed to be done and then do it.

Since 1985 my associates and I have worked with about ten thousand employees in over thirty companies, from as many as two thousand at New Jersey Bell to a total staff of thirty-five at Harris Graphics. We've worked with a diverse range of organizations, including almost half the Bell Operating Companies; the Copps Corporation, a wholesale and retail grocery chain in Wisconsin; Kondex, a small manufacturing company; and Lands' End, the direct-mail merchandising company.

The last eleven years have been an exciting journey, a continuing process of realization and creation. I have learned more and more about beliefs—how they are created and how to eliminate them. When I first developed the Lefkoe Belief Process (LBP), I really didn't know how or why it worked. I only knew that beliefs disappeared and patterns changed. I now have a much better understanding of TLM, which consists of the principles on which the LBP is based. After each private session and corporate assignment, I am always thrilled and somewhat awed by the results. Today, TLM continues to evolve.

Why I Wrote This Book

For several years I had been thinking about writing a book. Over time I had developed some theories that explained why TLM worked. As a result I realized what made it so effective at producing rapid and permanent change. And, most importantly, I developed TLM, a set of principles that can be used to make fundamental changes in individuals, organizations, and institutions. I finally had something to write about that could make a real difference in people's lives.

So, I faced a new challenge: How to write about TLM in such a way that it would become real for readers. I wanted people to understand that there was a brand-new possibility in their lives, to realize that they need not be stuck in old patterns that held them back and made aspects of their lives dysfunctional. But I was very clear that my work was not in the realm of self-help. My book could not be compared to books in that category. TLM is unique. Many books offer advice about how to cope with problems—at work, at home, in organizations, and in society. Instead, my work provides a technology and a process that enable people to *eliminate* their problems totally by eradicating the beliefs that are their source.

This book is the result of several years of grappling with how to explain TLM and how you can use this to recreate your life, transforming yourself and your world. I urge you to read it in the spirit of awakening and discovery. It can be the first step on the most exciting journey you've ever taken.

Part One

The Lefkoe Method Difference

Chapter 1

Is Profound Change Possible?

There is now incontrovertible evidence that mankind has just entered upon the greatest period of change the world has ever known. The ills from which we are suffering have had their seat in the very foundation of human thought.
—Pierre Teilhard de Chardin,
The Phenomenon of Man

As you look at the world, you may feel despair about the human condition. It seems impossible to solve the deeply embedded problems of crime, poverty, drug abuse, prejudice, and violence. The real problems never seem to get solved; in fact, they get worse as they are endlessly carried from generation to generation.

Imagine for a moment a different kind of society—one where people live in mutual respect and caring, working together to make a better life for everyone in the community. Imagine corporations that value creativity and collaboration above ego and greed. Who wouldn't want to live in a world where there was peace, supportive communities, and a deep commitment to freedom, happiness, and opportunity for everyone?

Now look at your own life. You too might have some problems, and sometimes they seem as insoluble as the big problems of the world. Maybe you've honestly tried to make positive changes, through therapy or self-help programs or other methods, because you really want to make your relationships work, do well at your job, be an effective parent, and really enjoy your life. But you keep slipping back into familiar patterns, and you can't figure out what to do. Why can't you consistently achieve what you think you should be capable of achieving?

You are no doubt reading this book because you are seriously committed to making changes, but you haven't been able to attain what you most passionately want—for yourself, your family, your company, and your community.

You wonder, "What's wrong with me?" "What's wrong with the world?" "What can I do about it?"

Something's Wrong

Perhaps one or more of the following scenarios will strike a familiar chord.

You Wake Up in the Morning Feeling Depressed

Well, maybe you're not exactly depressed. It's just that you've lost much of your enthusiasm for life. You realize that you are tired much of the time and it's getting harder to summon enough energy to do what has to be done.

Maybe you're not always tired; instead, you're frequently sad or anxious or angry. If you're like many people, however, you have some uncomfortable emotions that you'd rather not have. But you don't know why you have them. And even if you do, you don't know how to make them go away.

You Feel Out of Control

You remember the argument the night before with your spouse. What were you arguing about? The details are hazy; you only remember that it was a repeat of so many evenings when you said something, your spouse said something and before you knew it you were fighting. You try to control your temper, but something always sets you off.

Maybe there was no actual argument last night because you or your spouse just withdrew and refused to discuss the issue.

Maybe your anger was directed toward your children or coworkers, not your spouse. In any case, if you're like many people, you either experience and express your anger too frequently or you suppress it and burn inside. You don't know why. Or if you do, because you've undergone intensive therapy and soul-searching, you are stymied by your inability to change your behavior permanently.

Your Motivation Is Missing

You finally pull yourself out of bed. As you walk across the room you notice your reflection in the mirror and cringe. You remember your resolution to exercise three times a week. You look at the clock and see that you have time to walk on the treadmill for twenty minutes, but unaccountably you find yourself resisting. You know you should, but it's just too much trouble—which is what you've said every morning since you bought the treadmill several months ago.

Maybe it's not the treadmill, it's the stair climber. Maybe it's not the exercise, it's the diet. Most people have something they know they should do and really want to do, but they are never able to get around to it.

The World Is a Mess

As you start getting dressed, you turn on the morning news. The budget battle is still in progress. The Republicans say one thing, the Democrats say another, and meanwhile no solution really seems to work. You hate to be cynical, but it seems hopeless. Why, you ask yourself, do all the proposed solutions to a growing number of societal problems create as many problems as they solve? Why do so many problems seem insoluble?

Your Job Is a Rat Race

You arrive at work and are immediately called into a meeting. Another customer survey has come up with the same old message: They want better service or they'll take their business elsewhere. This is beginning to sound like a broken record that no one is able to fix. You've tried everything—giving bonuses to the service people, sending them to customer service training, even hiring new people to replace the ones who weren't working out. Although the level of customer satisfaction has risen somewhat, most of the service people don't really listen. They fix the machines or answer the questions, but their response to customers is lackluster and incomplete. They don't recognize the value of finding out what the customers want and need and then providing it.

Maybe it's not the service people. Maybe it's the managers, who continue to act like autocratic bosses, even though the company has encouraged them to be partners and team players. Or perhaps it's the hourly workers who resist working in the teams you've recently created. Whoever it is, virtually every organization has at least one group of employees who are resisting the changes needed to survive in today's hotly competitive global markets.

You Are Exhausted at the End of the Workday

You drag yourself home and walk in to find your kids glued to the TV set. You're instantly annoyed. The kids seem to spend more time watching TV and fighting with each other than studying, doing chores, or playing nicely. They're really good kids, but you're concerned that they're developing bad habits that will hurt them later in life. You've tried talking to them, explaining, yelling, and disciplining. You've tried rewarding them and threatening them. Nothing seems to work. Maybe you're doing something wrong, but what? This parenting business is harder than you thought.

You may have related to one of these scenarios or to all of them. There are literally hundreds of everyday scenarios in which you, the organization you work for, and the institutions on which you rely all do things that clearly won't work and appear to be unable to do things that obviously *will* work. What's worse, all too often there don't appear to be any viable solutions.

Could that *really* be the case, that there are no solutions to the myriad problems we face? Or is there some way to get control over our lives?

A Promise of Possibility

If you feel trapped in a world and a life that aren't all you would like them to be, I invite you to explore an entirely new way of dealing with reality. The principles and the process associated with The Lefkoe Method will allow you to discover:

- Why so much of your life doesn't work the way you want it to.

- How you can use a new set of tools to help you resolve each problem presented in the foregoing scenarios, along with the many others you experience daily.

- How you can join with others in transforming institutions and organizations so they really work.

I created TLM after many years of observing that people couldn't seem to accomplish what they wanted to. They were unable to initiate and then sustain positive change. Many of my clients have spent countless hours and dollars pursuing self-improvement. The corporations I advise usually have excellent executives and are constantly getting advice from competent consultants. The parents I know are always trying new ways to help their children become responsible, caring, and happy human beings. The problem isn't a lack of commitment to positive change. It's an inability to initiate and sustain it. Moreover, even if things look better for a while, the results are short-lived. Clearly, the old methods aren't working. Many people have come to realize that they need an entirely new method of examining problems and creating possibilities, but they have little idea where to look for such a method. The result can be a deep cynicism bordering on despair that has infected individuals, parents, companies, and organizations in our society—a sense of "What's the use? Things will never change."

Yet life is not hopeless; it is only that we have been looking in the wrong places. I have found, as a result of my work with individuals and organizations, that TLM enables people to achieve results that they never imagined were possible.

The tools of TLM help people eliminate virtually any dysfunctional emotional or behavioral pattern. They can enable drug and alcohol addicts to recover quickly and permanently. They can cure bulimia or anorexia for good. They can reform teenage and adult criminals. They can enable people to make fast, effortless, and lasting changes in long-held behaviors and emotional patterns, including phobias, prejudice, hostility, and chronic depression. They can rejuvenate sluggish corporations and prepare any organization to make the radical adjustments needed for our rapidly changing environment. They can enable institutions to truly serve the people who depend on them.

This seems like an awfully big promise, doesn't it? But I have seen it happen again and again, and I'll give you many case histories that will make the possibility of transformation real for you: Diane, whose bulimia was ruining her life before she eliminated the need for it; Barry, a hardened street criminal who broke the cycle of violence; Frank, who transcended the disease of AIDS. I'll also take you inside major corporations where TLM enabled the previously impossible to become possible. And finally, I'll show you how even the most tenaciously stubborn institutional problems, such as those that pervade our current education and health care systems, might be dissolved.

TLM is not another form of psychotherapy. It is not a self-help program like so many others that have been tried and have failed. Nor is it a motivational system to jump-start organizations. TLM is a paradigm-shifting approach that allows individuals and organizations to re-create themselves by eliminating the beliefs that cause them to behave in self-defeating, self-destructive ways and limit their ability to change.

Not Another Psychotherapy

Many of the individuals I work with as clients have spent some time in psychotherapy, and a number of my business clients have retained consultants for advice on how to change. I admire them for that, because it shows that they are eager to be more effective in the world. But I have also seen that even after years in therapy, trying self-help programs, and receiving lots of excellent advice, these clients are still stuck with their old, ineffective behaviors. Maybe they got better for a while, but it's rarely permanent.

By the time they come to me, they are understandably skeptical about trying TLM, but they are intrigued when I explain that it is not psychotherapy. Individual psychotherapy, most group therapies, and self-help programs enable people to cope much more effectively with their problems, but they are rarely capable of producing fundamental, lasting change. Even when they do, the struggle and the effort usually don't totally disappear.

There is a good reason why people are usually unable to get rid of dysfunctional behavior by using conventional methods. The principle implicit in most attempts to change behavior is: Information + Motivation = Change. This makes perfect sense to most people, whether they are psychotherapists, training professionals, parents, or individuals. If you know what to do and how to do it, and if you are motivated (positively or negatively), isn't that all you need to take the appropriate action?

Obviously not, since the formula doesn't seem to be working. If it were, everyone would wear seat belts, which they don't. Everyone would keep New Year's resolutions, instead of letting them go after a couple of weeks. People suffering from cardiovascular disease would all adopt low-fat, low-cholesterol diets. Corporate training programs would be effective in changing worker behavior.

Let's take a simple example. Say you're a procrastinator. You always leave work projects until the last minute. As a result, you're anxious much of the time and sometimes you turn projects in late, which subjects you to the disapproval of your boss. In fact, he tells you, "I'd like to consider you for a promotion and a raise, but I can't as long as you continue to deliver projects late." You decide you must change, and you really *want* to change. What do you do?

- You prioritize your activities, assuming that it will help you focus on the most important projects.

- You make a schedule that helps you allot time during the month for work on the project.

- You put up reminders in prominent places.

- You create rewards to give yourself when you finish a project—a special dinner or a new item of clothing.

- You ask your friends to support you.

So now you've gathered all the information and resources you need to get your projects done on time. And you have several strong reasons for doing it: a possible promotion, a raise, your boss's approval, an alleviation of your constant anxiety.

But be honest! After you've done all this, plus all the other variations you've discovered, does the behavior pattern really change? Does the Information + Motivation enable you to sit down easily and do what you say you are going to do? And if it does today, does it continue to be easy month after month? For most of us, the answer is no. (If you think this isn't a valid assumption, consider all the times you've made a similar commitment, buttressed by Information + Motivation, but for some in explicable reason you failed to follow through.)

Let's look at another example of how Information + Motivation is ineffective in helping people change their behavior and emotions. Perhaps you find yourself constantly worrying about what other people think of you. That's common enough. You've found that your ever-present concern with the opinions of others is annoying, at best. You want to change. You think that if you can rid yourself of this obsession, you will be a lot happier and more comfortable in social situations. So what do you do?

Maybe you begin by trying to appreciate your own value and to realize that your self-worth is not dependent on the opinions of others. You think about all the people who *do* like and appreciate you. You realize that the desire to be liked by everyone is self-defeating as well as impossible. Maybe you try to convince yourself that people who don't like you just aren't "your kind of people" so it doesn't really matter.

But don't you find, even with all your positive thinking and all your efforts, that the need to be liked by everybody doesn't go away? The reason is simple: *Information + Motivation aren't enough to change emotional and behavioral patterns because there are beliefs underneath the patterns that cause the problems and if those beliefs are not eliminated the problem will not go away.* The formula of Information + Motivation does not deal with beliefs. Therefore, the lasting change you were looking for is not possible.

Unfortunately, because most people believe that Information + Motivation *should* be enough, we usually blame ourselves or someone else when it doesn't work. We think, "I'm incompetent," or "She'll never learn," or "What's wrong with him?" When you depend on this formula as a reliable way to modify your behavior, it tends to end up as an invitation for failure, guilt, and blame.

With psychotherapy, you run into many of the same issues. Many forms of psychotherapy attempt to change behavior directly by using either logic or persuasion, ignoring beliefs altogether. One of the major forms of psychotherapy employed today, however, is cognitive therapy, which does focus on changing beliefs. That might sound like what I am doing, but it is actually very different. Let me explain.

Cognitive therapy is designed, first, to help you identify irrational beliefs and then to talk you out of them with reason and logic. The premise is that once you see your belief is illogical or self-defeating, you will be able to eliminate it. But what if your dysfunctional beliefs are not irrational at all but are a logical conclusion of an early experience? Here's an example.

Assume that you are a two-year-old child, the third of four. You have a brother and a sister, two and four years older than you, and a baby brother. Your parents never yell at you or hit you. Your dad works all day, and your mom stays home to take care of you and your siblings.

When you wake up in the morning, you jump out of bed and you say, "Mommy, Mommy, play with me. Paint with me. Read to me." And Mommy, with a four- and a six-year-old running around and a new baby, replies, "Not now, honey. I'm busy. Play by yourself or with your brother and sister for a while."

So, you go off to explore the house, and an hour or so later you come back to Mom and say, "Mommy, Mommy, play with me. Paint with me. Read to me." This time your mom says, "Not now, honey. I need to feed the baby. Maybe later."

Imagine that this scene gets repeated every hour or so until 6:00 p.m. when Daddy comes home. You rush to the door and yell, "Daddy, Daddy, look at what I made today!" Daddy replies, "Give me a minute until I can get my coat off and relax."

Eventually, Dad spends a few minutes with each of the kids, reads the paper, and watches TV which is followed by dinner. If all goes well, maybe Mom and Dad read to you and your siblings for a while before bedtime.

So, what happened on this typical day of your life at age two? You asked for attention fifteen or twenty times, and almost always you heard, "No, not now." Even if we were conservative and said you asked for attention only three times a day, that would mean about a thousand requests in a year that were usually denied, and four thousand separate denials by the age of six. What meaning would you give the experience with your mom and dad?

If you're a typical child, you might conclude (unconsciously) **I'm not important.** That would be a brilliant feat of integration for a child. You have had thousands of separate incidents that you didn't understand and that upset you. But deciding **I'm not important** now allows you to make sense of them. If you're not important, of course Dad and Mom wouldn't have time for you.

Say you carry this unconscious conclusion into adult life (which is usually what happens), and at some point a therapist provides you with a host of logical arguments to demonstrate you are important and it makes no sense whatsoever to believe otherwise. But it does make sense to you because you formed the belief as a reasonable interpretation of your experience.

Moreover, the "evidence" that you offer for a belief is not usually the real reason you believe it. Your evidence usually consists of recent observations that appear to substantiate the belief. The real source of your belief, however, is your interpretation of circumstances earlier in life.

For example, if you were to form the belief **Relationships don't work** as a child, you would act consistently with it thereafter. You might avoid relationships altogether. You might stay in a bad relationship thinking, I'll never find a better one. You might not try to talk to your partner in an attempt to make your relationship better. These and similar activities will produce current evidence for the already-existing belief. In other words, life becomes a self-fulfilling prophecy. Because the evidence you present to validate your beliefs is a consequence of the beliefs, not their source, challenging the validity of the evidence usually doesn't help.

Another form of psychotherapy is based on the idea that by fully experiencing "incomplete" episodes from your childhood, you can release them and eliminate their impact on you. The idea behind this type of therapy is that if you can release the experiences leading to your perception **I'm not important** they would be relived and virtually exorcised.

The problem with this method is that the source of dysfunctional behavior is not the early experiences themselves but instead, the beliefs you formed as a result. The experiences themselves do not have a lasting impact on you; after all, you don't live in the past, you live in the present. You can't go back and change experiences you've already had. But the beliefs that you form as a young child do have a significant impact—and you *can* change those.

Some psychotherapists, especially psychiatrists, who are medical doctors, focus on eliminating the symptoms of your problem, thinking that the illness *is* the set of symptoms. Perhaps your belief **I'm not important** results in symptoms of depression, and a psychiatrist recommends an antidepressant medication. You take the drug and you feel less depressed. Although your symptoms are alleviated—at least while you are taking the drug—the source of your depression has not disappeared and is likely to be manifested in other ways. (A dysfunctional behavioral or emotional pattern that clearly has a physical cause is an exception. But I believe those to be relatively rare.)

No wonder after many years of therapy or self-improvement courses, you're still struggling with the belief **I'm not important**.

Are you beginning to see why psychotherapy is limited? While the goal of psychotherapy is to help you cope better with your problems—and it frequently does that very well—*my* goal is to help you eliminate the problems totally, by eradicating the beliefs that are at the source. Many different psychological explanations of human behavior may be valid in that they are logical interpretations of why people behave the way they do. But they aren't particularly useful as tools to empower people to experience total satisfaction, eliminate dysfunctional patterns rapidly and permanently, and experience themselves as the creators of their lives, with infinite possibilities and no limitations. Nor are they useful in the broader and more profound sense of eliminating suffering in the world, reducing crime and violence, or creating effective institutions.

TLM is more about *creation* than about psychology. It's more spiritual than psychotherapeutic. When you eliminate a belief using TLM, you don't merely think, feel, and behave differently. You also enter what appears to be a non-ordinary state of consciousness. In this state you experience yourself as calm, serene, powerful, and alive. The possibilities of your life seem unlimited.

You experience that you have no limitations. Finally, there is no negative pattern to slip back into because your old beliefs no longer exist.

Are You Limited by Your Beliefs?

The core of TLM is that it enables you to eliminate the beliefs that lead to dysfunctional patterns. As you'll discover, your beliefs have an enormous power in your life.

What do you mean when you say you believe something? That it's true. A belief is a statement about reality that you think is "the truth," and this belief molds your behavior, your emotions, and your attitudes.

Each of your beliefs serves as a box that limits and determines the behavior that is possible for you.

Here's an example. Let's say you really believe that **Relationships don't work**. If that's your belief, your behavior would probably include one or more of the following actions:

- You wouldn't let people get close to you.

- You wouldn't try to work out problems in your relationships.

- You would spend a lot of time alone.

- You wouldn't allow superficial relationships to become close ones.

- You would stay in an unsatisfactory relationship without trying to change it.

Can you see that the belief **Relationships don't work** makes it almost impossible for you to sustain a satisfying relationship over a long period of time? If you eliminated this belief, wouldn't the behaviors just listed change automatically and naturally?

Consider another example of how your beliefs determine your behavior. Assume you held this belief: **The way to succeed in life is to avoid mistakes.** Although this belief would not necessitate any specific behavior, it would undoubtedly limit your behavior in one or more of the following ways:

- You would avoid taking chances.

- You would do the same thing, day after day, believing that if it worked yesterday it will work today.

- You would be more interested in assigning blame for a mistake than in finding its source and correcting it.

- You would respond defensively to criticism.

Behavior that is incompatible with your belief—like being open to criticism or taking risks—would be highly unlikely. Your behavior occurs in the box defined by your beliefs.

Usually, there are many beliefs that contribute to the patterns in your life. Anna, a client of mine, described her pattern in relationships as "fear of taking chances, shutting off." Just a few of the beliefs that contributed to this pattern were: **Relationships always end with someone getting hurt; there's something wrong with me; if I express my affection for someone, I'll get hurt.** The patterns in Anna's relationships could be explained by these and other related beliefs.

Beliefs Shape Your Emotions

Not only do your beliefs determine your behavior, they also determine how you experience things emotionally. For example, if you believe **Dogs are friendly,** the appearance of a boisterous, excited dog that jumps at you will produce delight and joy. But if you believe **Dogs are dangerous,** the same action by that same dog will produce fear. Change the belief, and your emotional reaction to the same stimulus automatically changes. This occurred with one of my clients. Larry had a phobic fear of crowds that led him to tremble, break out in a sweat, and hyperventilate whenever he was in the midst of one. "I don't know why I respond this way to crowds," he told me. "It's not rational."

As I worked with Larry, he discovered that his emotional reaction was based on the belief, **In a large group of people I don't know, something bad will happen.** When the belief was eliminated, Larry's fear went away, along with all of the accompanying physiological symptoms.

Many people have difficulty with the idea that emotional reactions are based on beliefs. They think of emotions as uncontrollable impulses, resulting from physiological and chemical changes that are separate from the mind. Feelings "just happen." TLM offers proof of a very different stance: Emotional reactions, or feelings, usually are very much dependent on beliefs.

Consider the emotional response you have to another person. Say you know a person named Fred whom you don't like very much. But a friend of yours does like Fred and feels very close to him. How can your reactions to Fred be so different? You may assume that you and your friend are observing different qualities in Fred, but in fact your friend probably sees the same qualities you do. The difference in your emotional response to Fred is a result of different beliefs the two of you have about people and friendship.

Fred is a very extroverted, gregarious person. Since your friend believes people should express themselves freely, he admires these qualities in Fred. On the other hand, you believe that people should be more reserved and only express themselves fully to very close friends. You don't like these qualities in Fred.

Fred's qualities are the same for you and your friend. Your different reactions result from the different beliefs you have about what those qualities mean.

Your beliefs determine your attitudes, which are a combination of what you think and how you feel. An attitude is an emotionally held belief. If you believe **I'm worthwhile; things usually work out the way I want them to; I can do whatever I**

really want to do, you will have a positive, optimistic attitude about life. On the other hand, if you believe **I'm not worthwhile; life is too hard; I'll never get what I want;** those beliefs will tend to give you a negative, pessimistic attitude about life.

Another example of attitudes caused by beliefs is racial, religious, and gender prejudice. Early in life many people form negative beliefs, such as: **Blacks, Jews, homosexuals, or women are inferior**. Such beliefs lead to prejudicial behavior toward these groups. Many people, as adults, feel uncomfortable or even guilty about their attitudes and behavior, and they try logically to talk themselves out of their feelings. Usually, however, they are unable to get rid of the attitudes and the subtle behavior associated with them—unless they eliminate the beliefs that are responsible for the prejudice. I have worked with several people who presented prejudice as their unwanted pattern. When the beliefs underlying the prejudice were eliminated, it totally disappeared.

These sessions were so successful that I believe TLM would be equally valuable in eliminating ethnic conflict between Serbs, Muslims, and Croats in Bosnia and between Israelis and Palestinians in the Middle East.

You Perceive What You Believe

Not only do your beliefs determine your behavior, your feelings, and your attitudes, they also determine what you are able to perceive. Everybody senses the same thing, but *perceiving* it is different. An over simplified description of how you see is that light strikes an object and is reflected in your eyes. Electrical impulses travel from the retina to the visual cortex, where the shape and color of the object are registered. But before you can actually see *an object*, electrical impulses have to travel from your visual cortex to your frontal lobe, where the sensation of sight is integrated into a perception of a specific, recognizable form. In other words, *sensations* are the raw data provided by the senses; *perceptions* are the result of what the brain does with the raw data. And *that* is largely a function of your beliefs. So it might be appropriate to reverse the old saying "I'll believe it when I see it" to the more accurate statement "I'll see it when I believe it."

Let's use a simple example. When you see white moisture on the ground in winter, you say, "That's snow." If, however, you asked an Eskimo man what he saw, he would point to as many as ten different places in the snow and use a different word to refer to each place. The Eskimo might ask you as he pointed, "Do you see the *kanevvluk* or the *muruaneq*? And, over there, the *natquik* and the *nutaryuk*?"[1] And you'd say, "No, I don't see any of that. I only see snow."

Are there really ten different "things" out there? There are for the person who has distinguished them, but not for the person who hasn't. It might not be hard to learn to distinguish ten different types of snow, but until you did, you would sense what the Eskimo senses, but you would not perceive what the Eskimo perceives.

Once you "see" something—or, more accurately, distinguish it—it really does exist for you, and you can no longer "not see" it. Consider the popular optical-illusion books that are filled with images you can only see after you soften your focus and look at the image without deciding what you expect to see. Once it comes into focus and you "see the picture," you can't stop seeing it.

Another example of how beliefs determine perception can be found in hypnosis. This is an altered state of consciousness in which it is possible for a hypnotist to make suggestions to a subject that the subject then believes while under hypnosis. One common trick is for a hypnotist to drop a $100 bill on the floor and tell a hypnotized man from the audience that it is his to keep if he can pick it up—*and* that it weighs one thousand pounds. The subject struggles mightily, yet fails to pick up the bill. Why? Because he believes it weighs one thousand pounds and thus, perceives it that way.

Eliminate Beliefs and Open Possibilities

When you eliminate the beliefs that are limiting you, you create new possibilities for action. You have the potential of discovering workable solutions that literally did not exist to you before. You are no longer limited by the box you were previously in.

Randy, one of my clients, described the following pattern to me: "I have a hard time seeing a project through to its completion in the accepted way. I keep getting stuck. When it starts getting close to the deadline, I just panic. I'm afraid if I don't come through I'll lose my job. So I end up taking shortcuts and cheating."

For many years, this was Randy's typical behavior, and he got by with it. But eventually his boss started noticing his shortcuts and cheating and told him he had to change his ways if he wanted to keep his job. Suddenly, Randy's behavior was a problem for him. He tried to follow the rules, but he was filled with fear that his projects wouldn't succeed. Eventually, he reverted to old patterns, despite his sincere desire not to.

My work with Randy focused on identifying the beliefs that accounted for his pattern of behavior, including **I can't do what's expected of me**.

I asked Randy, "Can you see that your behavior is absolutely consistent with that belief?" He realized that it was virtually impossible to change his behavior without first eliminating the belief.

Using TLM as you will find it described in Part Two, Randy began to eliminate the beliefs that were stopping him from finishing projects without cheating. When all of the beliefs were gone, he was able to complete projects successfully without cutting corners.

There is good news and bad news. The bad news is that the negative beliefs you have created in your life will create your reality. The good news is: The beliefs can be eliminated. After you eliminate a belief that has been driving unwanted behavior and discovered that *you created it*, you realize that you are the *creator* of your life. When you see that you create your life through your beliefs, you see that you can change your life by eliminating unwanted beliefs.

You Can Also Change the World

TLM is very effective on a personal level. But it is not merely a new self-help technique. Its ultimate implications are far more profound. Imagine a technology that has the power to change entire institutions so they continually operate in the most effective manner possible. Even if you believe that personal renewal is possible, it may be hard to picture such a Utopian view of society. It becomes easier when you understand that organizations and institutions have belief systems too—and their dysfunctional strategies and operations spring from these systems.

What people do in organizations is a function of the "culture"—the beliefs about what it takes to survive and succeed. These fundamental beliefs are manifested in innumerable policies, procedures, organizational structures, management styles, and systems.

Institutions operate out of a paradigm—a set of core beliefs—about their nature and purpose. All behaviors and actions flow from these basic beliefs, which shape the strategies of the institution.

In the same way that many individuals get stuck with dysfunctional and limiting beliefs, institutions and corporations also create boxes that prevent them from healthy operation and growth. They may try hard to solve their problems, but the more they try, within the framework of the box, the more deeply embedded the problems seem to become. As you will see in Part Three, what I call Third Order Change—being in a state of continuous creation—allows any institution and organization to devise workable strategies to deal with problems as they occur.

Before you can fully grasp the nature of TLM and learn how to use it, you must understand its underlying principles. These principles are fundamental. They reach back into the very nature of human consciousness.

Chapter 2

Principles of TLM

The basic structures of the material world are determined, ultimately, by the way we look at this world ...the observed patterns of matter are reflections of patterns of mind.

—Frijof Capra,
The Turning Point

*T*he *principles* of TLM are based on a theory about the nature of consciousness, creation, and reality—specifically, how our consciousness creates reality by making distinctions.

I ask you to set aside every preconceived idea you hold, just for a moment, and consider a different way of viewing life. Begin with these five principles:

1. Existence is a function of consciousness.

2. Language is the primary tool we use to make distinctions.

3. There is no inherent meaning (or truth) in the world.

4. When you create a belief, you create your reality.

5. When you eliminate a belief, you change your reality and create new possibilities.

Let's explore these points in more depth.

1. Existence Is a Function of Consciousness

If you ask someone, "Do things exist?" the response would probably be, "Of course things exist! The world is full of things." Doesn't everyone know that there is physical stuff out there—that reality is tangible and real?

But what allows any *thing*—a hand, a chair, or any other object—to exist? One way to answer is to imagine a specific thing—say, a hand. What if the hand expands and keeps expanding until there is nothing in the universe except the hand? What would happen to it? You wouldn't see the hand anymore. It would disappear because there would be nothing in the universe that was not the hand. This is a very basic concept about reality: In order for any *thing* to exist, there must also be not that thing.

Consider this for a moment. Can you see that any physical object is bounded by "not that object"? If an object did not have any borders—that is, if it wasn't surrounded by "not that object"— it couldn't be distinguished from everything else. In other words, it wouldn't exist.

The same principle applies to nonmaterial concepts. Love and hate, peace and war, strong and weak, beautiful and ugly— these only exist and have unique attributes because they have been distinguished from each other. For example, the state of war is distinguished from peace by the presence of armed conflict. When there is no armed conflict there is peace. But if armed conflict existed throughout the world all the time, and if the alternative (peace) was unimaginable, you wouldn't be able to distinguish war from any other state. War, as a condition distinct from peace, couldn't exist.

Now imagine everything in the universe without any distinctions. It's all just an undifferentiated whole. Can you see that there is no*thing*? That's because in order for *anything* to exist, it must be distinguished from everything else. If no distinction is made between a specific thing and everything else, there is only an undifferentiated everything—which is another way of saying *nothing*.

Everything, without any distinctions, is the same as nothing.

Physicist Fred Allen Wolf once said that "the world is only a potential and not present without you or me to observe it." I would suggest that what physical reality really requires is consciousness to make distinctions.

In making distinctions, we use our sensory apparatus (the five senses) as well as our perceptual framework (language, culture, paradigms, and individual beliefs). But the world isn't really the way you perceive it. It isn't *any* way until you perceive it that way—that is, until you distinguish it that way. In fact, you don't even sense what is "out there" because there is *nothing* out there to be sensed. (No*thing*, as we've seen, however, is the potential for everything to be distinguished.)

An example comes from a *Time* magazine cover story on human consciousness.

A baby born with cataracts—an unusual but not unheard-of condition—and left untreated for as little as six months becomes permanently and irrevocably blind. If a sixty-year-old develops cataracts, an operation can restore full sight. The distinctions most of us make unconsciously and at a glance—foreground vs. background, moving vs. stationary, vertical vs. horizontal, and dozens more—are concepts that the brain has learned. It literally has to wire itself, with neurons growing out to touch and communicate with one another in an ever more sophisticated network of connections. And if those connections are not repeatedly stimulated in the first few months of life, when the brain is still in its formative period, they atrophy and die.[1]

In other words, moving and stationary or vertical and horizontal are not events "out there." Rather they are concepts that the brain has learned (or distinguished) as a result of having a specific sensory apparatus, without which they couldn't be distinguished. In this case, these concepts would not exist.

2. Language Is the Primary Tool We Use to Make Distinctions

What we perceive is also determined to a large extent by our personal beliefs, which are largely a function of our culture and our immediate environment. Our most important tool in making distinctions and creating our reality is language.[2]

As Edward Sapir, a noted anthropologist, has said:

Human beings do not live in the objective world alone, or alone in the world of social activity as ordinarily understood, but are very much at the mercy of a particular language which has become the medium of expression for their society. The fact of the matter is that their "real world" is to a large extent unconsciously built up in the language habits of the group. . . . We see and hear and otherwise experience very largely as we do because the language habits of our community predispose certain choices of interpretation.[3,4]

Language is far more than a tool for communication. The word "language" comes from *logos*, which means category or concept. With language we categorize, distinguish, and create how we see and understand the universe. Ultimately, we perceive the world according to our language. For example, when we think in English, we perceive a world made up primarily of objects: people, trees, houses. These objects do things or have things done to them using verbs. We *see* everything in the world in this fashion. We don't perceive "things out there" because there really *are* things out there. That just happens to be our worldview, because in our language there is a *subject*, which acts upon an *object*, which exists independently of the subject. In the English language, independent entities (subjects and objects) are primary, rather than processes or relationships. That's not true in every language.

As Ralph Strauch points out in his book *The Reality Illusion*:

Some languages are structured around quite different basic word-categories and relationships. They project very different pictures of the basic nature of reality as a result. The language of the Nootka Indians in the Pacific Northwest, for example, has only one principle word-category; it denotes happenings or events. A verbal form like "eventing" might better describe this word-category, except that such a form doesn't sound right in English, with its emphasis on noun forms. We might think of Nootka as composed entirely of verbs, except that they take no subjects or objects as English verbs do. The Nootka, then, perceive the world as a stream of transient events, rather than as the collection of more or less permanent objects, which we see. Even something, which we see clearly as a physical object, like a house, the Nootka perceive of as a long-lived temporal event. The literal English translation of the Nootka concept might be something like "housing occurs," or "it houses."[5]

In a discussion of this point, Larry Dossey quotes Nobel Prize winning physicist Werner Heisenberg as saying:

What we are observing is not nature itself, but nature exposed to our method of questioning. And how do we question? All of our methods of interrogating nature depend on language—and it is the very nature of language to refer to things. We therefore think in terms of things. How can we possibly think of nonthings, nothings, nothing? In our very *forms* of thought we instinctively divide the world into subjects and objects, thinkers and things, mind and matter. This division seems so natural that it has been presumed a basic maxim of objective science.[6]

3. There Is No Inherent Meaning ("The Truth") in the World

If nothing exists without distinctions, then there are only interpretations and no inherent meaning in the world. For example, you have never seen anywhere in the world that "I am [anything]," or "Life is...," or "People are..." You have never seen anything beautiful or ugly, good or bad. You see people behaving and talking, and you see objects acting on other objects (such as acts of nature), but you have never seen the meaning of any of these behaviors or events. If I ask you, "Have you ever seen a comfortable chair?" you might reply that you have. But have you *really*? No. You have only seen a chair, which you *interpreted* as being comfortable. Other people might interpret the chair as being uncomfortable. "Comfort" is not inherent in chairs.

Your beliefs, including the negative ones that you might hold about yourself, such as **I'm not worthwhile,** usually stem from your experiences as a child. You might think they are "facts" that existed in the world before you "discovered" them. But your beliefs are not facts; they are interpretations of what you see and hear. For example, if as a child you watched your parents fighting a lot instead of expressing signs of love and affection, you might have concluded, **Marriage doesn't work**. That belief was formed in your mind as a child. It was an interpretation of what you heard and saw. It became "the truth" for you, but it was never really the truth. There were other ways to interpret what you observed, such as, **My parents' marriage doesn't work, but others might.** Or, **Some relationships work and others don't.** Beliefs are single interpretations that we make based on how we, individually observe events. You didn't *see* your belief in the world. You only saw one couple arguing. Your interpretations don't exist in the world, only in your mind.

There is an old story attributed to author Karl Weick about three baseball umpires discussing their job. The first one says, "I calls 'em like they *is*." The second one says, "I calls 'em like I *sees* 'em." And the third one says, "There ain't nothin' *there* until I calls 'em."

Once you make a distinction and bring some*thing* into reality, it is difficult to imagine that thing not existing. It really *does* exist for you. Reality, for any given person, can be described as that which that person's consciousness has already distinguished.

4. *When You Create a Belief, You Create Your Reality*

When you realize that you never saw your beliefs in the world, that you only saw events that had no inherent meaning, it becomes clear that you create your beliefs—and, ultimately, your reality. Thus, everything we say is "out there," other than what we touch, see, hear, smell, or taste, is a distinction we create that exists only in our mind.

Creation is the act of making distinctions. For example, you walk down the street and think you *see* "men" and "women" when you actually only perceive individual human beings. You describe these human beings as "men" or "women," but you have never actually seen "men" or "women." You see abstractions that you have distinguished. If you were to arbitrarily distinguish people into those taller and those shorter than six feet, you would eventually walk down the street and think you are seeing "shorties" and "tallies" as clearly as you now see men and women.

In *Alternate Realities*, Lawrence LeShan gives a simple example:

> Consider how we make classes of things. "Surely," we say, "we do not *create* classes. We take them as we find them 'out there,' male and female, animal, vegetable, and mineral...We are not creating anything. We are observing things and learning their relationships." Why then, asked one philosopher, has no one made a class of red, juicy, edible things and included meat and cherries in it? Or a class of tall, dark-haired men and women with no earlobes?...It becomes clear, as we look at these trivial points, that...we help create and maintain the reality we perceive and react to.[7]

So nothing is until you make it so. But once you do, it *must be*. You can no longer *not see* men and women.

Here is a vivid example. In *The Experts Speak,* by Christopher Cerf and Victor Navasky, hundreds of experts are cited who were limited in their ability to see anything outside their existing beliefs. The following is just one of the beliefs that was generally accepted as "the truth" and that determined the believer's behavior at the time.

Cerf and Navasky tell of how in the 1850s, a Hungarian doctor and professor of obstetrics, Ignaz Semmelweis, ordered his interns at the Viennese Lying-In Hospital to wash their hands after performing autopsies and before examining new mothers. The death rate plummeted from 22 out of 200 to two out of 200, prompting the following reaction from one of Europe's most respected medical practitioners, "It may be that it (Semmelweis' procedure) does contain a few good principles, but its scrupulous application has presented such difficulties that it would be necessary, in Paris for instance, to place in quarantine the personnel of a hospital the great part of a year, and that, moreover, to obtain results that remain entirely problematical." (Dr. Charles Dubois, Parisian obstetrician, in a memo to the French Academy, on September 23, 1858.)

Semmelweis' superiors shared Dubois' opinion. When the Hungarian physician insisted on defending his theories, they forced him to resign his post on the faculty.[8]

In modern times, we may view this example as ridiculous. Doesn't everyone know that proper hygiene is a lifesaving factor in hospitals? We tend to view this as an objective reality—a fact. But Dubois and his colleagues were operating out of a different worldview, from a different set of beliefs. Semmelweis' theory did not fit with their beliefs about hospital care, and therefore it was not the truth for them.

The only thing that is "true" is that which you make true by definition. You create reality (truth) by making arbitrary distinctions out of nothing. Whatever you distinguish becomes real (true) by the very fact of your having made the distinction. The distinction brings some*thing* into existence. It also serves as the definition of what has been brought into existence. The world is— but only because we said so. We are, by our very nature, conscious beings who distinguish, which means beings who create "reality."

Once you have created a belief, you have created a reality in which your belief is "the truth." And your life becomes consistent with that belief. You have constant evidence that the belief is true. You have a hard time even imagining possible behavior that is not consistent with your belief. It is difficult to eliminate or change the belief because you feel as though you actually perceive it existing in the world. So your behavior continues to be consistent with your belief, even if it is dysfunctional and you try to change it.

I like to use this story as an illustration. Imagine God saying, "Let there be Earth, with land and water," and there was Earth with land and water. Then God said, "I think I'd like to visit Earth and go sailing all around the planet." So God goes to Earth, creates a boat, gets in it, and starts sailing. After a while, however, even God would not be able to continue sailing because the boat would bump into land. Obviously God could make the land disappear and continue sailing. But as long as there is land, which God created, even God could not sail unimpeded around the world.

5. When You Eliminate a Belief, You Change Your Reality and Create New Possibilities

Because things only exist as a result of distinctions you make, when you dissolve or eliminate the distinction that reality disappears. The following exercise demonstrates my point.

Let's distinguish a two-dimensional figure with three straight sides from every other possible figure and call it a triangle. (A definition is nothing more than how you describe a specific distinction.) Now let's change the figure by adding one more side and making it a four-sided figure with equal angles. Notice you no longer have a triangle. You now have a figure we have defined as a rectangle. The new figure no longer fits the definition of a triangle. You might say that the triangle has disappeared. It doesn't exist. From this illustration we learn that when the unique attributes of a "thing" are changed, and when the distinction that makes it unique from other "things" is changed, it disappears.

This principle explains what makes a belief disappear during the LBP. In the LBP, you identify a specific belief, which is a conviction you have. This belief is characterized by your particular way of viewing the world. For you, it is "the truth," as distinguished from all other views, which are not "the truth." You then transform a statement that you consider to be "*the* truth" into a statement that you consider to be "*a* truth." Once you do this, the statement is no longer a *belief.* It is now an *interpretation*—one of many possible ways of defining reality. Thus, the belief no longer exists. It has disappeared. And when the belief is gone, your reality has changed. Now new possibilities appear that weren't there before.

Most therapies assume that there is an objective world "out there" that the individual is having trouble dealing with. Therefore, the conventional role of therapy is to help people cope better with that objective world.

TLM on the other hand, assumes that there is no "reality" independent from your beliefs. Thus, altering your beliefs not only changes your behavior, your feelings, and how you perceive the world, it literally changes the world in which you function.

TLM is a way to use these philosophical principles in everyday life. We think that our beliefs about education, healthcare, the penal system, parenting, business, and so on are "the truth." Our problem-solving strategies are consistent with our (often unconscious) beliefs. And because we think we have discovered our beliefs in the world, they are very hard to let go of, and we strongly resist strategies or ideas that are inconsistent with them. But once we see that our beliefs are merely interpretations or distinctions we made—and not "the truth" at all—we are open to other alternatives.

Before you can eliminate a belief, however, you have to be able to identify what it is you believe and how you arrived at that belief. That's the next point in our discussion.

Chapter 3

What's Holding You Back?

Whether you say you can or you can't—
you're always right!
—Anonymous

Your core self-esteem beliefs are formed early in childhood. In many ways, these beliefs shape who you are and are thus, very influential in determining how you deal with the world.

Many medical experts, psychologists, and parenting authorities agree that possessing self-esteem is the key to living as empowered adults. A major government task force that spent three years studying self-esteem concluded:

> Self-esteem is the likeliest candidate for a social vaccine, something that empowers us to live responsibly and that inoculates us against the lures of crime, violence, substance abuse, teen pregnancy, child abuse, chronic welfare dependency, and educational failure. The lack of self-esteem is central to most personal and social ills plaguing our state and nation as we approach the end of the twentieth century.[1]

Many people have a sense that these conclusions are true, but it is unclear what the specific relationship is between self-esteem and how we live our lives. So, we might ask, "Why does poor self-esteem lead to dysfunctional behavior and emotions?"

In my own experience, after having worked with thousands of people, I found that negative self-esteem beliefs were at the root

---

of almost every dysfunctional pattern of emotion or behavior that people presented.[2]

For example:

- Beneath Ron's inability to express his feelings was the belief **I'm not lovable.**

- Beneath Sally's fear of confronting people was the belief **I'm not worthy.**

- Beneath Barney's avoidance of relationships was the belief **I'm not good enough.**

Martha came to see me just after she left a long marriage in which her husband had been cold, physically detached, and emotionally abusive. She wanted to understand why she hadn't left him earlier. During her session, Martha realized that she experienced herself as someone who wasn't worthwhile. One of her beliefs was **I'm unworthy.** At that point, it became clear to her that the reason she hadn't left her husband was that she hadn't felt she was worthy enough to have someone who would treat her better. Her cold, abusive husband was "just what I deserved."

Martha then recalled that shortly before her marriage she had briefly dated a man who was very warm and loving and who had treated her "like a queen." She remembered feeling uncomfortable with him, so she broke off the relationship. What she wasn't conscious of at the time, but realized during our session, was that she'd been afraid that he would "find out I wasn't worthy and leave me." Soon after she broke up with him, she met the man she eventually married. Even though he treated her badly and she never felt he loved her, she stayed with him for thirty years.

Martha's self-esteem belief—**I'm unworthy**—created a reality in which she experienced no choice but to live unloved for thirty years. It's a startling example of the impact low self-esteem beliefs can have on your life.

But how are self-esteem beliefs formed?

In the Beginning

At birth, you are in a state of unlimited possibility. You don't enter the world with a tag on your foot that defines you as a specific type of person with a predestined set of beliefs and patterns. You're just consciousness—the creator of the creation you will become.

Into that vacuum of pure possibility comes your environment, your circumstances, and the behaviors of others. You begin to create distinctions about what you experience. Those distinctions become your beliefs. For example, my client Laurie was rarely able to get her parents to accommodate any of her desires. Everything was always done *their* way. By the age of six, after consistently having her wishes denied and being urged to go along with what her parents told her, Laurie formed the belief **I don't matter**, and she felt and acted according to that belief. Had Laurie been able to interpret her parents' behavior to mean that **My mom and dad don't have very good parenting skills**, she would not have gone through life with that belief, even though her parents had behaved the same way. This latter conclusion would have been a huge and likely impossible leap of understanding for a small child; that's why so many of the beliefs formed in childhood result in low self-esteem. In fact, it is typical of children to blame themselves for their parents' behavior. Children believe that adults are all-knowing. If their parents ignore, criticize, punish, or abandon them, they assume it must be their own fault. Children are also totally dependent on adults for survival, so it's scary for them to think adults don't know what they're doing. Therefore, it feels safer to interpret the behavior of their parents as their own fault. It was natural for Laurie to form the belief **I don't matter** as a result of her parents' behavior.

Parents Don't Cause Our Beliefs

It is important to clarify that although Laurie's parents were the source of her belief, they were not the *cause*. As the creator of her beliefs, Laurie made that distinction herself. Her parents' behavior merely constituted the circumstances that she observed while she was creating the belief in her own mind.

It is important to realize that beliefs about yourself are not merely thoughts inside your head. Once a child makes these distinctions, they actually *become beliefs*. So when Laurie concluded **I don't matter**, she actually became someone who felt she didn't matter. Her actions, perceptions, interpretations, feelings—and even the way she was treated—became consistent with being someone who didn't matter.

We create our lives based on models (such as our parents), but those models have no inherent power to cause us to believe anything. Consider this metaphor. A painter bases his painting on a model, but you wouldn't say that the model created the painting. Clearly, the painter created it, although it would have been a different painting had there been a different model. In the same way, other people do not create you; they are merely models from which you create yourself.

Just as a painter might change his work or dab away a color that isn't acceptable after the model has left, you can change your beliefs any time after you leave the environment that was your model.

The Consequences of Negative Self-Esteem

It makes all the difference in the world how you create yourself. Let's assume that you create one of the two following sets of self-esteem beliefs: **I'm not good enough**; **I'm not okay**; **there's something wrong with me**; **I'm not worthwhile**; **I don't matter**. Or: **I'm good enough**; **I'm okay just the way I am**; **I'm worthwhile just because I am, not for any reason**; **I matter**.

Which set of beliefs would most likely lead to anxiety and depression? To substance abuse? To teenage pregnancy? To eating disorders? To satisfying relationships? To a productive career?

It may seem obvious, but many people get stuck with the idea that these are not beliefs at all—they are expressions of ego or "who I really am." I use the term "ego" here to mean who you think you are: namely, the collection of beliefs, feelings, and behaviors that you use to identify yourself and to distinguish yourself from others. For example, you may describe yourself as a good parent, a loving spouse, a compassionate person, or a hard worker.

People often say that certain behaviors or attitudes are "just the way I am" or "part of my personality." Conversely, you might say, "That's not me" or "I'm just not that kind of person." People box themselves into an identity as if it were an objective thing. In reality, one's "identity," like everything else, is a result of distinctions they made and therefore, can change. It wasn't just given to them at birth. In other words, they experience themselves as the *identity* or *creation* when really *they did the creating*.

During my first few sessions with Barbara, she would acknowledge a dysfunctional pattern, such as hostility, and then say, "That's me. That's just the way I am." Her sense of herself and her behavior was consistent with the beliefs and behavior she had formed early in life. She defined them collectively as "me." After Barbara eliminated several beliefs, she discovered that they didn't define her at all. Her experience of herself changed totally.

When you experience yourself as your ego, you are limited by the specific beliefs with which you have identified yourself. For example, if you say "It's not safe to express myself," or "I'm not artistic," you feel and live consistently.

Your ego isn't who you really are. It is merely who you think you are and therefore, experience yourself as being. Who you really are is *the creator of your ego*. Remember, you start life as a blank slate with unlimited possibilities. Then, as the creator of your beliefs, you form the conclusions about yourself that ultimately constitute your ego. You experience yourself as that which got created and easily forget that you really did the creating all along.

You are not the sum total of your decisions. You are the decision maker.

Creating a Survival Strategy

Let's say you are a young child who has created a host of negative beliefs about yourself or about life. At this point you are in school, interacting with other kids and adults. You are beginning to realize that you are going to grow up and will have to make your own way in life. You are confronted with a real dilemma, albeit an unconscious one: "How will I make it in life if there's something fundamentally wrong with me or the world?"

Imagine the fear and anxiety you must feel when you experience these two conflicting "facts." On one hand, your experience is **I must make it on my own in life**. On the other hand, you have concluded **There's something fundamentally wrong with me.**

Fear and anxiety are unpleasant and painful feelings, so children who have them try to find ways of not feeling them. During sessions using the LBP, I've discovered that people have two basic ways of dealing with the unpleasant feelings that are caused by negative self-esteem beliefs: Either, they use alcohol, drugs, food, or other substances to cover up the feelings and numb themselves or to make themselves feel good. Or, they develop survival strategies:

I'm good enough if/because...

What makes me worthwhile is...

The way to deal with a dangerous world is...

The way to survive is...

Survival strategy beliefs are based on a child's observation of what it takes to feel good about herself or himself, to be important, to be worthwhile, or to be able to deal with life.

For example:

> Susan's parents placed a heavy emphasis on friendships, on what others thought of them, and on impressing people, so Susan concluded that the way to survive was to get everyone to like and approve of her.

> Art lived in a community where the people who were considered important and given respect were in gangs and carried guns, so he chose that as his survival strategy.

> Jennifer discovered in high school that boys sought out the attractive girls who wore makeup and nice clothes, so Jennifer concluded that the way to win approval was to look pretty.

Once you decide that a positive sense of yourself is "because of" anything, you've created a lifelong problem. If you say the only way to be good enough is to be wealthy and have a big house, your sense of worth is linked to that goal. If you aren't wealthy and don't have a big house, you are forced to face your belief that you're not good enough. Moreover, even if you achieve your survival strategy, there's the danger of losing it. Total disaster is always just around the corner for you. Life becomes a sea of anxiety, in which you are constantly struggling to meet the conditions you have made for being good enough. Your self-esteem is always in question.

Tom, an executive in a Wall Street firm, earns over $200,000 a year. His core belief is **I don't matter**, and his survival strategy belief is **What makes me worthwhile is being seen as important by others**. As a result, Tom becomes anxious whenever a new person gets hired, or a colleague wins praise, or he isn't included in a meeting, or his boss doesn't acknowledge him after he's completed a project.

Miriam has the survival strategy belief **Being beautiful makes me acceptable**. For most of her life, she has lived comfortably with that belief. Her beauty earned her quite a bit of attention, admiration, and even love. But now Miriam is approaching fifty, and she's frightened. The march of time is threatening to rob her of the one thing that she believes makes her acceptable. She has become increasingly depressed; every time a man fails to look at her admiringly, she feels as if she doesn't matter.

One consequence of being run by survival strategy beliefs is that instead of living out of choices and pleasure—doing things because you want to do them—you do them primarily to survive. You experience your survival as dependent on the success of your survival strategy. The need to fulfill the terms of your survival strategy dominates your life.[3]

Someone once said, "You can never get enough of what you never really wanted in the first place." That's an excellent description of trying to live with survival strategies formed to compensate for negative self-esteem beliefs. Once you say you're not worthwhile just the way you are, no amount of accomplishment or praise will provide the unconditional sense of self-esteem you want and need.

People who have beliefs that are indicative of low self-esteem are not just criminals or drug addicts or unsuccessful people or those who suffer from deep depression. Many people with low self-esteem are visibly successful, living in nice homes with stable families. What distinguishes people is not their self-esteem beliefs, but their survival strategies—the ways they cope with a negative sense of themselves.

Jonathan, a businessman, concluded **What makes me good enough is getting away with things I shouldn't do** to compensate for the belief **I'm not good enough**.

Sandy, a mental health professional, used **What makes me okay is taking care of other people** to help her deal with the belief **I'm not okay**.

Charlie, a financial executive, concluded **What makes me valuable is getting results** to cover up the belief **I'm not important**.

Although the dysfunctional behavior that people exhibit is usually a direct result of their survival strategy beliefs, the energy that drives the survival strategies is the underlying negative self-esteem. Thus, both the underlying self-esteem beliefs *and* the survival strategy beliefs have to be eliminated. The role of survival strategy beliefs explains why therapies designed to improve self-esteem rarely produce fundamental and lasting changes in people's lives.

True Self-esteem Is Unconditional

Don, a top executive in his company, spent an hour of our first session describing how many corporations wanted to hire him as CEO, how wealthy he was, and how many business successes he had. But, as we worked together, Don discovered something that truly astonished him. First he discovered the belief **I'm not worthy**, which was his interpretation of why he had received very little attention from his parents. Then he remembered that when he was a child his parents only gave him positive attention when he exceeded their expectations. He formed the belief **What makes me okay is exceeding people's expectations**. He grew into a driven workaholic, accumulating wealth, success, and acknowledgment along the way, but never really feeling he had done enough. His belief kept him running on all cylinders, but there was little satisfaction or joy in his success. And while others observing him might have said that Don was a man with very high self-esteem, in fact he never felt good about himself.

Self-esteem is not conceit, arrogance, or bragging. Acting important or trying to convince others you are important is not a behavior characteristic of a person with high self-esteem. It is a manifestation of a survival strategy—in Don's case, the need to convince himself and others that he was okay.

Positive self-esteem is a fundamental sense of yourself as okay just the way you are. It is created unconditionally. You are good enough just because you create yourself that way—not because of anything you do. You can't earn self-esteem. For example, if you get straight A's in school and your parents never acknowledge your good marks—or constantly point to what you *haven't* accomplished—you may form the belief **I can never do anything right**. On the other hand, if you get poor grades, yet your parents offer unconditional love, try to support you in your studies, and praise you for those things you do well, you probably won't develop negative self-esteem beliefs. It isn't achievements or grades that are responsible for self-esteem.

Praise and rewards won't necessarily lead to high self-esteem. In fact, children who receive indiscriminate praise might tend to look outside themselves for acceptance instead of trusting their own judgment.

The crucial issue is how children interpret any given set of experiences, which is determined by all their other experiences, the beliefs they have already formed, and the fact that they are only children. In chapter 9, I will offer parents some techniques for enhancing self-esteem in their children.

Being the Creator

As long as you are going to have an ego, you need positive self-esteem—the sense that the creation you have created yourself to be is able and worthy of surviving in the world you have created.

At any given moment, it's possible to experience yourself either as *an ego—a specific set of distinctions or beliefs—or the creator of your life—who creates the distinctions.*

People who use TLM significantly change their sense of themselves by eliminating dysfunctional beliefs. If they do it repeatedly, they also are able to take the experience of being the creator into their everyday lives. They have a sense of "nothing missing," of satisfaction, of not being at the mercy of difficult circumstances. They seem to be living both as the ego they have created and, at the same time, as the creator of the ego.

For example, from time to time my wife does or says something and I get angry. I used to think that my anger was *caused* by Shelly, and I would stay angry at her for hours or even days. Now I still get angry sometimes (although not as often), but my immediate reaction isn't that Shelly *caused* my anger. As the *creator*, I observe that I am reacting to something Shelly did or said. I watch "Morty the creation" being angry and I ask, "What does he believe that makes him so upset?" Sometimes I find a belief, and sometimes I don't. I don't try to talk myself out of my feelings or try to suppress them. I fully experience them. Yet, almost always I also experience a distance between "myself" and the reaction, and I realize that the reaction isn't being caused by Shelly. So I am not run by my anger, I rarely react to it, and I am able to get over it quickly.

A metaphor I use to describe this state is that life is a game (such as Monopoly) that we think is real. Most people live as if they are the Top Hat—going to jail, collecting $200, paying others for landing on their property, and so on. But after you have created and then experienced yourself as the creator several times, you experience that you aren't the Top Hat. You are, instead, both the creator of the game and that which is moving the Top Hat around the board.

Moreover, when you play Monopoly, you are excited about passing GO and disappointed when you land on someone else's property or get sent to jail. But you usually have the sense that it is just a game that you'll be putting away in a few hours.

When you experience yourself repeatedly as the creator of your life, you feel that way about life: There are incidents that feel good and those that feel bad, circumstances that turn out the way you want and others that don't. But there is always the clear sense that life is a game—to be played all-out but at the same time not taken too seriously. You experience that life has *already* turned out; there is no place to get to. Whatever is happening is a function of beliefs you created—and you can eliminate them at any time. You realize that you created your world and therefore, you can change it.

Part Two

The Lefkoe Method in Action

Chapter 4

How TLM Works

No great improvements in the lot of mankind are possible until a great change takes place in their mode of thought.
　　　　　　　　　　　—John Stuart Mill

You may have had the following experience with self-help exercises. You read an exercise in a book that is supposed to help you "work through" some problem—like an inability to have satisfying relationships or being overweight. You decide to try the exercise on yourself. Maybe you write answers to questions, or practice positive thoughts, or follow specific steps. You do this trusting that the formula of the exercise will produce the results you're seeking if you do it correctly. Self-help books are full of these exercises, and at best they help you in the short-term. Rarely, if ever, do they produce profound and lasting change.

As you will see in this chapter, TLM does. It usually requires a trained facilitator. That's mainly because the beliefs that need to be eliminated are not known. They are usually unconscious, and assistance is required to identify all of the beliefs responsible for any given problem. However, as I will demonstrate in chapter 5, once you know the beliefs you want to work on, you often can use a modified version of the LBP to eliminate unwanted beliefs in your own life, with your children, or with friends.

In Part Three I will demonstrate how TLM can be used for large-scale transformation in institutions and organizations. For now, just concentrate on grasping the steps of the LBP.

The Lefkoe Method

There are seven steps to the LBP:

1. Identify the undesirable pattern.

2. Name the underlying beliefs.

3. Identify the source of each belief.

4. Describe other possibilities (alternate interpretations).

5. Realize you didn't "see" the belief in the world.

6. Eliminate the old belief.

7. See yourself as the creator.

I've chosen my client Joan to help illustrate how the process works. Joan, an attractive and soft-spoken professional woman in her mid-forties, came to see me after hearing a speech I'd made about TLM. She thought I might be able to help her. Joan had been a government worker for twenty years and had recently left her job to try and start her own business. She confided that she had been divorced for five years, after spending ten years in a "horrible" marriage, and she still felt resentful about the way her husband had treated her.

Step One: Joan's Undesirable Pattern

I asked Joan to describe an undesired pattern that she wanted to change. She told me, "My problem is that, while other people have confidence in me, I never feel as good about myself as others do. I'm afraid to challenge people, afraid to take a stand. I'm always doing more for others than they do for me." She paused. "I guess you'd call it low self-esteem. In a way, I feel that my life is a fake. Some days I don't even get out of bed because I'm so depressed."

"Is depression the pattern you want to work on?" I asked.

She nodded. "Yes. It's been getting worse since I left my job. I want to start a business, but I have a sense of just not caring."

Step Two: Joan's Underlying Beliefs

I explained to Joan that everything we do and feel is a function of our beliefs. "What do you believe that could account for your depression?"

"I have a lot of negative beliefs about myself," Joan responded readily. "**I'm not good enough. I'm not worthy.** And a lot more."

"What seems the most real right now?"

She thought a moment. "**I'm not worthy.**"

"Can you see that the belief **I'm not worthy** would at least partially explain your pattern, your depression and negative sense of yourself, your sense of 'Why try?' 'Why care?' 'Why get out of bed?'"

"Yes, I can see that," she agreed.

Step Three: Finding the Source of Joan's Belief

I then asked Joan to look for the circumstances or events that led her to form her belief. As we have seen, fundamental beliefs about yourself and about life (the kind of beliefs that shape your self-esteem) are usually formed before the age of six, based on early interactions with parents and other primary caretakers. Beliefs are almost always formed by a pattern of events, not just a single incident.

When I asked Joan to think about what happened to her as a child that might have led to the belief **I'm not worthy**, she told me about growing up on a ranch in Texas that her father ran. "I had a brother three years older and a sister ten years younger. We lived way out in an isolated area. There was no one to play with, so I always played alone. I was a loner. I never had any approval as a child. I remember thinking if I had party clothes it was so my parents could impress the neighbors. They seemed to be very worried that I not embarrass them.

"My parents were very much in love with each other. My father was always buying Mother something, but not me. I didn't see much of him. I never really knew my father.

"My mother was always telling me to 'be a good girl.' But, she never praised me or said loving things to me. I wasn't criticized, I was ignored. She never hugged or kissed me or told me she was happy I was her little girl or that she loved me no matter what. If we displeased her, she burst into tears. I'd feel rotten. Father was always trying to please her, but I never could. I had the sense that if I did something that was really embarrassing, I'd be banished."

I had been listening without interruption for some time. Now I said, "I think you've found the source of your belief. Does it make sense to you that what you've just told me about your childhood is the source of the belief **I'm not worthy**?"

Joan's face was very sad. "Yes."

"Can you see that the conclusion you reached that **I'm not worthy** made a lot of sense to a four-, five-, or six-year-old girl? That it wasn't silly or stupid or off-the-wall?"

She nodded.

"Can you also see that you were a little girl, trying to understand hundreds of different upsetting, confusing experiences with your mom and dad? And they just didn't make sense, until one day you said—probably not consciously—'if **I'm not worthy**, everything makes sense. My parents' behavior makes sense.'"

"I can see that."

"And that's what you believed to be the truth. You didn't make a mistake. You made the logical conclusion any child in your place would have made."

Step Four: Describing Other Possibilities

"Let's play a game called Possibilities," I said. "You start with a set of experiences. We'll use the ones you just told me from your childhood. Then I'll ask you to make up as many different explanations or interpretations of those experiences as you can. You've already made one interpretation of your parents' behavior toward you. You concluded **I'm not worthy**. What might be some others?

Joan labored hard over her list and finally came up with six other ways to interpret her parents' behavior:

1. My parents treated me the way they did because they thought I wasn't worthy, but they were wrong.

2. My parents' behavior had nothing to do with me. They did what they did because of their beliefs from childhood.

3. My mother didn't know how to be a good mother and show love for her children.

4. My mother was frustrated about being stuck out on the ranch, and she took it out on me.

5. I wasn't good enough by my mother's standards, but I might be by other people's standards.

6. My mother didn't have a very effective parenting style. It wasn't my fault.

"Good." I smiled at Joan. "Can you see that each of these statements could explain your parents' behavior just as well as the conclusion you reached as a child that you weren't worthy?"

Joan had tears in her eyes. "Yes," she said quietly.

I then asked Joan, "is what you have been living with as 'the truth' about you since you were a little girl only one arbitrary interpretation made by that little girl?"

"That's right."

Step Five: Joan Realizes She Didn't "See" the belief in the World

"If you try to picture yourself back on the ranch, didn't it seem to you that you could see right in front of you, almost like it was a physical thing: **I'm not worthy**? It was probably the most real thing in your childhood."

"Yes, it was," she agreed.

"Did you really *see* it? Was it out there in reality to be seen?"[1]

She smiled ruefully. "No. It was an interpretation. I made it up."

"Okay, if **I'm not worthy** wasn't out there in the world, where was it?"

"In my mind."

"And what did you actually see in the world?"

"I saw my parents' behavior."

"Do you notice what happened?" I asked Joan. "Even though **I'm not worthy** was never the truth, once you said it you lived your life as if it were the truth. You felt that way and tried to compensate for feeling that way; it determined your behavior. You even found a husband who treated you that way. Even though it's not 'the truth,' your life became consistent with the belief **I'm not worthy**.

"What if you had had an aunt whom you were very close to as a child, who saw everything that happened to you, and to whom you confided everything you were thinking. What if after you told her you were concluding **I'm not worthy**, you two had the conversation we just had today? Is it real to you that if she had helped you reach any other possible interpretation of your parents' behavior, your life would have been consistent with that conclusion? For example, if you had said your parents' behavior meant they didn't have good parenting skills and had nothing to do with you, would your life have been different?"

"Absolutely. I wouldn't have felt unworthy. I wouldn't have married the man I married."

Joan was silent. She looked stunned by this new realization.

Step Six: Joan Eliminates Her Belief

After a time, I said, "Look inside yourself, Joan. Look for that place where you felt **I'm not worthy** when we first started this session. Is **I'm not worthy** still the truth for you?"

She paused. After a moment, she replied. "No. That's not the truth. I'm not unworthy. It's just something I made up."

"Would you say that your belief **I'm not worthy** has disappeared?"

"Yes, it has."

"There are two ways of knowing that a belief has disappeared. First, you look inside and see the belief isn't there anymore. When you say the words of the belief out loud they don't feel true. That's what you've just done. Second, since a belief limits you to behavior that is consistent with it, if the belief goes away you should see new possibilities that you couldn't see before. I'm not asking you to predict how you will feel tomorrow. But can you at least imagine the possibility of waking up in the morning and *caring*? Of feeling worthy?"

"I still don't feel totally great about myself, but I can *imagine* it," Joan said.

"Could you have imagined that possibility an hour ago?"

"Definitely not."

"Joan, you only eliminated one belief today," I said. "It will never come back. Your childhood led to a lot of other beliefs that manifest themselves as depression. That's why you still don't feel great about yourself. By eliminating one belief, you created some new possibilities for feeling better about yourself that weren't there before. When you eliminate all the beliefs that are responsible for the depression—be they one or thirty—the pattern of depression will disappear. Don't invalidate what you did today. If you feel depressed, ask yourself if you still believe **I'm not worthy**. You won't. And if you eliminate the other beliefs, like **I'm not good enough**, which you mentioned earlier, ultimately your depression will lift totally."

Step Seven: Joan Sees Herself as the Creator

Eliminating the first belief was a huge breakthrough for Joan. Her entire life had been spent carrying around this negative belief about herself. It was like a giant boulder resting on her shoulders. Now she saw **I'm not worthy** was simply an interpretation. "I've lived with **I'm not worthy**, and it's not true." Once she realized that her belief was not "*the* truth," only "*a* truth," it disappeared. It no longer defined her. She no longer had to live her life as though she was someone who was not worthy.

Once you see that you are not your beliefs, but instead that you *create* your beliefs, you have tremendous ability to shape the direction of your life. This process gives you the ability to re-create yourself as a person who is able to eliminate negative beliefs and invent new possibilities for your life.[2]

Let's return to Joan. "You told me earlier that you were a person who was not worthy," I said. "But now you have eliminated that belief. You have discovered it wasn't the truth. But if you *are* your beliefs and the beliefs disappear, your sense of yourself should have disappeared. Look inside. Do you still experience 'Joan'?"

Joan laughed. "Of course I do!"

"Okay. If that's the case, you can't *be* your beliefs because one of your core beliefs disappeared and there's still 'you.' In fact, you could repeat what you did today with a hundred beliefs about yourself and you'd still experience a 'you' inside. Which leads us to the question: If you aren't the sum total of your beliefs and the behavior and emotions that stem from them, who are you, really?"

She looked totally confused. "Um. . . I am someone who *is* worthy?"

I smiled. "No, you just made that up. That's no more true than your belief that you weren't worthy. I'll give you a hint. How did the belief **I'm not worthy** get in your head in the first place?"

"My parents. What they did."

"No, that's what happened. How did what happened translate into your belief?"

"It's the way I interpreted it,' she said.

"Uh huh. So, do you see that before there can be an interpretation, there must first be an interpreter? There had to be someone who created the belief before there could be a belief? Can you see that you aren't your decisions, you're the decision *maker*?"

Joan smiled. "I am the interpreter."

"Yes." I sat back in my chair and regarded Joan. "Each of us really is the decision maker, not the decisions we've made. You can call that soul, or spirit, or consciousness, or whatever description you like. Another way to put it is that when you were born you were the possibility for all possibilities. Remember, Joan, your life has been consistent with **I'm not worthy**, even though this isn't and never was the truth about you. You realized that if you had said something different as a child, that other conclusion would have become the truth for you, and your life would have been consistent with it. You are the possibility for anything until you identify yourself as specific beliefs. Is that clear to you?"

"That's clear."

"Well, if your life is consistent with your beliefs, and you make up your beliefs, what does that make you?"

Her response sounded like a question. "The creator of my life?"

"Is that real to you?"

Her eyes widened and she sat back in her chair. She took a deep breath. "That's actually *very* real to me right now."

I explained to Joan that the only thing that is "true" is that which a person makes true by definition. We create reality by making distinctions. I asked her to consider the ways we "know" something. A crucial aspect of TLM is to know that you are the creator of your life in a very different way from how we usually "know" things.

This is the way I described it to Joan: There are three different ways of "knowing" something: (1) understanding it, using language; (2) experiencing it; and (3) creating it.

Consider knowing how to ride a bike. You can read about it, watch others do it, study the physics of balance, and be given detailed instructions. You can understand the mechanics of bike riding so well that you could tell someone else how to do it. But the kind of knowledge that consists of understanding is very different than the knowledge you get from experiencing it—getting on and falling off forty or fifty times until your body learns how to balance and you can ride a bike down the street.

We sometimes confuse our description of an experience with the experience itself because we communicate by using words. For example, let's say your friend describes a great meal he had at a local restaurant and you respond, "Oh, I know exactly what you're talking about." Maybe you "understand" what he's talking about, but you have not had your friend's experience. Understanding and experiencing are two different things.

There is a third way of knowing something. We are going to focus on this way in TLM. It's knowing something as a result of *creating* it.

I'm sure that on more than one occasion in your life you had someone teach you something—for example, how to solve a math problem. If your teacher was competent, you understood what to do. Moreover, once you had performed the math problem, you had experienced doing it. If you continued studying and learning, however, something very special might have happened to you. One day, you might have had a deeper sense of knowing, a flash of conceptual insight that allowed you to see the problem in a qualitatively different light. You thought, "Aha! That's what my teacher meant." After this experience, you "know" the material in a different way. You "own" your understanding; it's yours. In a sense, you did the same thing as the first person who ever solved the problem. You actively created the answer for yourself as opposed to just passively understanding the answer.

The distinction between these three ways of knowing— understanding, experiencing, and creating—is important.

After explaining this to Joan, I said, "At the moment in our conversation when you said, 'I didn't see **I'm not worthy** in the world, it was just an interpretation'—at the moment you realized that your interpretation only became true because you said so and that anything you would have said would have been true for you. At that moment, you created yourself as the creator of your life. If you look inside yourself, is it real to you that you not only understand and experience that you are the creator of your life, but you also know it in a different, more profound way?"

"Yes, I do," she said. "It's more like an intuitive knowledge. It's like I just know it and don't need reasons."

"Before we end," I said to Joan, "I'd like you to notice what it's like being the creator of your life. Would you say that no matter how good any given moment in your life has been, you've always had the sense that something was missing?"

She looked sad again. "Absolutely."

"Joan, just put aside for a moment what you've known to be true up until now and what you expect to be true when you leave. Look inside as the possibility for all possibilities, as the creator of your life. Is there anything missing right now, at this moment?"

She looked at me with an expression of surprise. "No. No, there's nothing missing."

"And what are you experiencing right now, as the creator of your life?"

"I feel good. Peaceful. Like a weight has been lifted off me. Powerful. There are no limitations. It's all up to me."

"What you've just described is the natural experience of human beings when they've created themselves as the creators of their lives. You've had a moment in that state. Imagine living your whole life that way."

Although Joan's belief **I'm not worthy** would never return and her pattern of depression would start to change immediately, I knew that the non-ordinary state of consciousness she was in would not last long after the LBP session. However, the more she created that state for herself in future sessions, the longer it would last. In time, the non-ordinary state of consciousness and the experience of unlimited possibilities would become a real and active part of her. She would begin to view her life as what the Buddhists call "a silent witness." She would "have" upsets, she would not be upset. She would "have" disappointments, she would not be disappointed. She would observe barriers in her life, but she would not be stopped by them. She would no longer experience herself as a victim of external forces. She would no longer experience herself as a player on the stage of her life. She would know in all these ways that she is the creator of the play.

A Profoundly Spiritual Process

As you think about Joan's experience with TLM, at first it may seem quite simplistic. But TLM is far more than merely understanding that your beliefs are interpretations and having them disappear. As I explained earlier, you know you are the creator because you have *created* it, not merely understood or experienced it. It involves creating yourself as the creator of your beliefs—and therefore as the creator of your life.

TLM is not about logical knowing and deciding. It appears, rather, to be a cognitive gateway to a non-ordinary state of consciousness in which you create and then experience yourself as okay just the way you are.

Imagine living in a state where nothing exists as inherently good or bad, where events have no inherent meaning—only the meaning you assign to them.

TLM lets you experience a profoundly spiritual state of consciousness. It is a reawakening. I want you to try to imagine the impact of the principles of TLM on your personal life, on your company, and on society.

We try to solve problems in our personal lives—as well as in education, health care, the penal system, parenting, and business—with strategies that are consistent with the (usually unconscious) beliefs we hold about those areas. Because we think we discovered our beliefs in "the world" and have evidence for them, we strongly resist any strategies or ideas that are inconsistent with them. When we realize, however, that we never "saw in the world" what we believe, but we only interpreted it, the beliefs disappear and we are no longer stuck in our preconceived ideas. We are open to other alternatives. This principle works for more than just personal use. By changing the cultures of organizations and the paradigms of institutions, it can also be used to solve problems in every area of life.

In the next chapter, I will give you suggestions about how you might employ the principles and some of the elements of TLM in your daily life. Then I'll walk you through several particularly moving case histories. When you read these stories—about how TLM transformed the lives of a bulimic woman, a young criminal, and a man with AIDS—you'll see just how unlimited the possibilities really are.

Chapter 5

Using TLM in Daily Life

It isn't until it is, and then it must be.
—Morty Lefkoe

Have you ever woke up in the morning, realized that you overslept, and cried, "**Today is going to be a bad day**"? I imagine most people have had that experience at one time or another. There are numerous occasions in life when you or those around you draw an immediate conclusion like that. At the moment, it seems very real—the only possible conclusion you could have reached under the circumstances. That conclusion, in turn, almost always becomes a self-fulfilling prophecy.

In these everyday instances, you can use an abbreviated form of the LBP to eliminate the belief before it has a chance to do any damage.

As you have seen, the steps of TLM are relatively simple. Once you realize that what you have lived with as "*the* truth" is only "*a* truth," that what you thought you "saw" in the world exists only in your mind as one arbitrary interpretation out of many, the belief disappears. TLM is not especially difficult to use when you know the belief you want to eliminate and its source—like **Today is going to be a bad day.**

The aspect of the LBP that usually requires intensive training is when a person is aware of a dysfunctional pattern that he or she wants to stop but isn't aware of all the beliefs that cause it. Finding the relevant beliefs and their sources requires skills that go way beyond merely finding possibilities for early events.

This explains why I have emphasized that this is not a self-help book. You may not be able to use TLM directly on yourself or even with friends, to address long-standing dysfunctional patterns. But, as this chapter will demonstrate, the modified LBP can be an invaluable tool in everyday situations when the belief is known.[1]

The following case histories demonstrate both the wide range of applicability of this modified version of the LBP and exactly how you can use it in your personal life.

Case 1. A Morning Belief: *Today Is Going to Be a Bad Day*

Let's begin with the initial example. How many times have you exclaimed in the morning, "**Today is going to be a bad day**," as a result of oversleeping, spilling coffee on your shirt, missing a bus, or not being able to get your car started? Probably more times than you'd like to remember. Although this belief relates only to the day it is formed, have you noticed how it manifests and becomes a self-fulfilling prophecy? How, as the day progresses, it is filled with things that go wrong? This situation is a perfect opportunity to use the modified LBP to eliminate a belief as soon as it is formed because you clearly know the belief and the events that led to it. Here's how you can do it.

1. What Is the Belief?

You know it because you just said it: **Today is going to be a bad day**.

2. What Happened to Lead to That Conclusion?

You turned the alarm off and went back to sleep. You were running late and then your car wouldn't start. As a result, you were late for work (or whatever your scenario is).

Can you see that your conclusion was a logical interpretation of the events that occurred—that what happened to you might well mean **Today is going to be a bad day**?

3. Are There Other, Equally Legitimate, Interpretations?

What are some other possibilities? What else could the events mean? Waking up late could also mean:

- You were very tired, which is why you went back to sleep, but after getting more sleep you're now in great shape for the rest of the day.

- The first event of the day was bad, but now that you've used up your share of bad luck for the day, the rest of the day will be great.

- Based only on what happened so far, the rest of the day might be bad or it might not be bad.

- The first event of the day has no connection whatsoever with the other events of the day.

Can you see that what happened in the morning could mean **Today is going to be a bad day**, but also could have these other meanings? Can you see that what you concluded to be "*the* truth" is only "*a* truth"—one of several possible interpretations of what actually happened?

4. Did You See It in the World?

Didn't it seem to you as if you could see with your eyes, right out there in the world: **Today is going to be a bad day**? It seemed like it, didn't it? Look again. You didn't really see it in the world, did you? You can't see into the future. What if you won the lottery that afternoon? Would it still be a bad day? So, if you didn't really see it in the world, where was the belief? Can you see that it was only in your mind, merely one interpretation of many?

5. Is It the Truth?

Is it true that **Today is going to be a bad day**? Do you still believe it? At this point the belief will have disappeared.

Case 2. A Child's Fear: Crowds Are Dangerous

When my daughter Blake was six, I worked successfully with her to find and eliminate a belief that was causing her a problem.

On many occasions, Shelly and I had taken Blake to fairs and shows where there were hundreds of people, and she usually enjoyed herself at these events. One Saturday we took her to a school that was having games, face painting, and a lot of other activities for kids. We had been inside only a few minutes when Blake screamed and exclaimed, "I'm scared! I want to leave!"

"What's wrong?" we asked her.

"I don't know. I'm just scared. I want to leave," she repeated.

We tried to find out what was scaring her, but she didn't know. The closest she could come to an answer was that there were a lot of people there. I reminded her that she had never before been afraid of crowds. What was it about this crowd that was so scary? She didn't know.

When we realized that the fear wasn't going away, we left. When we got home I sat down with Blake and asked, "Do you remember that Mommy and Daddy talk about the work we do with people in our sessions? How we help them with things that bother them in their lives?"

"Yes."

"Would you like me to try to help you figure out what is scaring you? You've never been scared of crowds before."

"Okay," she said solemnly.

We started trying to identify the belief. Blake named it almost immediately. **"Crowds are dangerous."**

"Okay, what happened that gave you that idea?"

She didn't pause even for a minute. "Remember when we went to the Italian street fair? Remember the lady who burned me with the cigarette?"

I certainly did remember. The fair had been mobbed; we could barely walk. We had been there for only a few minutes when Blake had screamed in pain. A woman had walked by her, swinging a lighted cigarette in her hand, and had hit Blake's arm with it. The woman then turned around, yelled at Blake, "Watch where you're going!" and walked away. Fortunately, the burn wasn't bad and Blake had wanted to stay for another couple of hours.

"So did you decide **Crowds are dangerous** based on your experience at that fair?"

"Yes."

"I can see why you concluded that. The idea makes a lot of sense. A lot of people would have said the same thing, honey. Now we're going to play a little game. What else could explain what happened to you other than what you said? It really could be that crowds are dangerous. But what else would explain what happened?"

She wasn't sure what I meant, so I said, "For example, *that* fair was dangerous, but maybe not all *other* fairs will be dangerous."

She got into the spirit of the game. I gave one interpretation, then she gave one:

- That woman didn't care if she hurt you, but other women would.

- People carrying lighted cigarettes can hurt me; people without cigarettes can't.

- That person wasn't careful with her cigarette, but most people would be.

- I'll get hurt at some crowded places, not others.

- The crowd at that fair was dangerous; other crowds wouldn't be.

- I'll get hurt at fairs, but not other crowded places.

- You have to be careful of people who have cigarettes.

Blake was having fun with TLM .

"Okay, honey," I said, "can you see that it made sense to conclude when you got burned that **crowds are dangerous**, but that there are a lot of other explanations for what happened?"

She understood what I was saying. She nodded.

I looked directly into her eyes and asked, "Didn't it seem, at the fair, right after you got burned, that you saw right in front of you that crowds are dangerous and that you'll get hurt?"

"Yes, that's what I saw."

"Is it clear now, honey, that you didn't see that, you only imagined that? You *did* see one woman burn you, but you never saw with your eyes that all crowds are dangerous. Did you?"

"I know what you mean, Daddy, I didn't see it. I only thought it."

Case 3. A Belief about Achievement:
I'll Never Get It Right

You can put the modified LBP to excellent use with sports. How many times have you missed a short putt, double-faulted, or thrown a bowling ball into the gutter? What did you feel? What did you think? Maybe you remember thinking to yourself, **I'm getting worse** or **I've blown it again** or **I'll never get it right**.

Pause now and remember feeling that way. Doesn't it seem as if you actually perceived that conclusion, that you actually observed in the world **I'll never get it right**? By now it should be clear that, in fact, you didn't discover any of these things out in the world. They are all interpretations of what you did observe—a ball that didn't go where you wanted it to go. This event was meaningless until you decided that it meant something. That is when you formed your belief. And then, once you believe **I'll never get it right**, guess what? It becomes true for you.

Get into the habit of watching your thought processes as you play sports. Notice when you interpret, when you judge your performance as good or bad. As soon as you do, stop for a minute and realize that you have just reached a conclusion (such as **I'll never get it right**) based on your interpretation of one or more events. Acknowledge that it is a valid interpretation; in other words, you *might* never get it right. And then come up with four or five other interpretations. For example:

> I had a single bad stroke, but it doesn't mean anything about my next strokes.

> I'm having a bad first hole (or first game), and I'll improve as the day goes on.

> I lost my concentration for a moment, and I'll get it right back.

> It's taking me a few minutes to get warmed up.

If there are at least four other interpretations of your performance that are just as good as the one you made, can you see that what you concluded is itself only an interpretation and not "*the* truth"? Is it real that you never saw your conclusion in the world?

If you practice this technique, you can eventually get to the point where you will catch yourself making a judgment and reaching a conclusion at the very moment it occurs. Then, as you begin to realize there is no meaning in the event, you can eliminate the beliefs as fast as they are created. It is possible to learn to distinguish between observations and interpretations on the spot.

Case 4. A Child's Struggle: I'm Stupid in Math

Sometimes your children (or friends) reach conclusions about themselves and life, and are very aware of those conclusions on a daily basis. It usually takes them only a minute to locate the source of the belief because it happened relatively recently. You can then help them make up several alternative explanations for the incident, and the belief will disappear.

Here's one real-life example. Shelly's former partner in her parenting business, Kim, has a daughter, Elizabeth. Shelly was at their house one day when Elizabeth, who was nine at the time, threw her pencil down while doing her math homework and exclaimed, "I'm stupid in math!"

Kim immediately asked, "Do you really believe that?"

"I sure do," she replied.

Shelly looked over at Kim, as if asking for her permission. Kim smiled and nodded. Shelly turned to Elizabeth and asked, "Where did you see **I'm stupid in math**?"

Elizabeth explained. "My teacher gave a surprise test in math a couple of days ago. I failed it. My teacher then put the names of everyone who had failed on the board. Everyone in the class saw who the stupid kids were."

"You're saying that your belief **I'm stupid in math** came from the incident with the math teacher a few days ago?"

"Yes," Elizabeth answered.

"That's a very reasonable conclusion," Shelly said. "In fact, a lot of the kids whose names were on the board probably concluded the same thing, didn't they?"

"I bet they did!"

"What else could that incident have meant? How else could you explain it?"

After a little coaching, Elizabeth came up with these possibilities:

- I wasn't prepared for that test, but if she had given notice and I had studied for it, I could have done well.

- I'm not good in math now, but I'll get better later on.

- I was tired that day, and I wasn't thinking well.

- It was a particularly hard test.

- It was a lot of times tables that we had to do quickly, which I didn't know, but that doesn't mean I'm bad in other areas of math.

- I had just gotten in a fight with another kid and I was distracted.

Shelly asked her, "Can you see that failing the test and having your name put on the board could mean that you're stupid in math—and it could also mean a lot of other things?"

"Sure, I can see that."

"Didn't it seem as if you could see **I'm stupid in math** in the classroom at the time?"

"I sure did."

"Is it real to you now that you never saw that and it was only one of several possible interpretations?"

"Yeah. I didn't see it."

"Is **I'm stupid in math** the truth?"

"No, it's not."

A few months later Elizabeth came home from school and excitedly told her mother, "We had a Mastery Test in math and I got an 'excellent'!"

Case 5. A Common Phobia: Flying is Dangerous

Have you ever had a scary experience on a plane and then concluded **Flying is dangerous**? (If not, think of another scary situation you experienced. We'll use flying for the purpose of this example.) This is a perfect example of knowing both a belief and its source, which enables you to eliminate the belief quickly and easily.

What happened that led to the belief? It could have been any number of things: A near plane crash, a very rough plane ride where it seemed as if the plane was about to crash, reading about a crash in which many people died, or another similar example. **Flying is dangerous** is a reasonable conclusion to form after any of these events. But what are a few other interpretations or explanations?

- That plane crashed (or almost crashed); it does not mean every plane flight will crash.

- Some planes crash (or almost crash); it doesn't mean every flight will crash.

- That particular airline isn't safe; it doesn't mean all airlines are the same.

- That particular pilot wasn't competent; it doesn't mean that all pilots are the same.

Didn't it seem as if you could see it with your eyes: **Flying is dangerous**? Did you really see that, or was that merely your interpretation of one specific event? If it was just one arbitrary interpretation that you never saw in the world, where was it?

Is it really "*the* truth?" Do you still believe it? Once you can see that the belief is not "*the* truth" and you never actually saw it, the belief will be gone.

Case 6. A Business Application: Our New Department Head Will Never Get This Department to Work

The modified LBP can be very useful in a variety of work situations, regardless of your position. For example, say there's been a proposed change at your company, and you're talking to a coworker who exclaims, "It will never work." You may agree, in which case the point is moot. But what happens when you disagree? You give all your reasons why you think you're right and your coworker is wrong. But how often do your arguments really change your coworker's mind? By now it should be clear that logical arguments usually fall on deaf ears. That's because they are heard through a filter composed of the sense that you "saw" the belief in the world. Therefore, no matter what anyone says, you are right and they are wrong. Try this instead.

Imagine your buddy George stops by your desk one afternoon and announces, "Our new department head will never get this department to work." Instead of trying to convince him that he's wrong, ask, "What happened that led you to that conclusion?"

He will no doubt begin telling you stories—about how no one could get the department to work in the past or about the prior failures of the new department head in other positions. Try responding like this: "With the facts you just told me, I understand why you reached your conclusion. It makes perfect sense, given that information. I wonder though, what are some other logical interpretations or meanings for the events you've just related?"

Some possibilities might be:

- No one has been able to get the department to work before; it doesn't necessarily mean no one will be able to succeed in the future.

- The conditions necessary to get the department to work haven't existed before now.

- No one else has had the support of management before.

- The new manager couldn't get other departments to work; it doesn't mean he won't be able to get this department to work.

- He wasn't the right person for the people who worked in the other places, but he might be the right person for this department.

- He didn't have the necessary skills before, but he's learned on the job what it takes to be a successful department manager, and he now has the necessary skills.

Ask your coworker, "Can you see that what you said is one logical conclusion, but that there are other logical conclusions as well? Doesn't it seem like, right now, you can see in the world that **Our new department head will never get this department to work**? But can you really see that in the world? Is it 'the truth' that **Our new department head will never get this department to work**? Can you see for sure into the future?"

Using this process can make a big impact on the day-to-day negative beliefs that get formed around the office.

Case 7. Totally Boxed In: Beliefs Can't Be Permanently Eliminated

There are many people who have a fundamental belief that real change is impossible. This might be stated as **Beliefs can't be permanently eliminated**.

If you have this belief it's probably because you have tried unsuccessfully to eliminate beliefs and behaviors at various times of your life. You might have tried psychotherapy, personal growth workshops, or on your own. You may have been told by psychotherapists that beliefs can't be permanently eliminated, or you may have read it in a book.

What other meanings could those experiences have?

- You haven't been able to eliminate beliefs with the technology you have used so far.

- The psychotherapists you have used were not successful; that doesn't mean other people won't be able to help you.

- People believe that because they have not found a way, but if they tried this technology they would not believe that.

- You didn't recognize that you never saw your belief in the world and that it was only in your mind and that is why they didn't go away.

- You weren't ready to eliminate a belief earlier in your life, but you might be now.

Hasn't it seemed as if you could clearly see in the world that **Beliefs can't be permanently eliminated**? Did you ever really *see* that? If you didn't see it in the world, if it's only been in your mind, is it really "*the* truth"? Do you still believe it?

I hear this belief in sessions from time to time. A person will eliminate a belief and then resist acknowledging that the belief has been eliminated. When I can see in the person's face that the belief is gone and they still can't acknowledge it, I use this quick version of the LBP. After the belief that **Beliefs can't be permanently eliminated** has been eliminated, the person is clear that the belief we had been working on really is gone.

Chapter 6

Case History Diane: Conquering Bulimia

Human beings, by changing the inner attitudes of their minds, can change the outer aspects of their lives.
—William James

You can now see that it isn't very difficult to eliminate a belief that is causing problems in everyday life *when you know the belief.* Most of the time, however, we only know the behavioral and emotional patterns that bother us, such as depression, anxiety, procrastination, and an inability to express our feelings. We usually don't know the beliefs that cause these patterns.

Exploring the patterns and identifying the appropriate beliefs that were formed in childhood takes more intensive digging and analysis. It's very hard for most individuals to do this kind of deep work for themselves. Usually our beliefs are unconscious, so people aren't even aware of them. In those circumstances, they might need a trained facilitator to help them go through TLM.

The case histories in the next three chapters are examples of that kind of complex work. Reading them, you'll begin to see that TLM is capable of finding the specific beliefs that are responsible for a given pattern—beliefs that people didn't even know they had—and then eliminating them, thereby changing dysfunctional patterns and creating possibilities that once seemed unimaginable. Reading about the experiences of these three very different people should put you one step closer to making real for yourself some of the concepts we've discussed. These case histories should also demonstrate how powerful TLM can be for everyone, regardless of their problems.

We begin with Diane. My work with her took sixteen sessions, spread out over more than a year. I've chosen her story to demonstrate how certain patterns of behavior, like bulimia, are not really what they seem to be. Bulimia is far more complex than one's relationship to food; it is intricately woven in with many self-esteem beliefs, survival strategy beliefs, and a negative sense of life developed in childhood. These must be brought to the surface and eliminated before the overt pattern of bulimia can be addressed.

This is one reason why "behavior modification" approaches usually don't create lasting change. It is almost impossible to really change one's behavior permanently if the beliefs that led to it still exist.

In the following recounting, you will begin to see how TLM can be used to eliminate a complex pattern. Be aware that during our time together, Diane discovered and eliminated many more beliefs than those detailed in the text. Often, in cases like this, a person needs to eliminate fifty or more beliefs. I have chosen those that best illuminate TLM and Diane's struggle.

Meeting Diane

Diane was sixty-three years old, a lovely, well-dressed woman with a warm, vulnerable face. She described her patterns as guilt, difficulty expressing her feelings, and bulimia. Diane told me quite frankly that she had low self-esteem.

Diane had been in a group to which I spoke briefly about TLM , but she didn't understand it very well. She was surprised when I avoided tackling her eating problem head-on. I explained that the beliefs responsible for eating and bodily illness are not usually as direct as the beliefs responsible for most behavioral and emotional patterns. Dysfunctional eating patterns are a survival strategy, so they usually involve not only beliefs about eating but also self-esteem beliefs. I suggested that we work on the other dysfunctional patterns in her life for a while before we directly addressed her eating problem. She agreed.

I began by asking Diane to identify several beliefs that could account for the inability to express her feelings. She immediately thought of one: **I'm not good enough.**

I asked her what might have contributed to this belief as she was growing up.

She told of a tormented childhood. "My family lived in a house with my aunt and uncle and two cousins," she said. "I was always compared unfavorably to my older brother and my cousins because I was different and had my own interests. From the time I was very small, I loved to paint and draw. My parents never accepted this; they thought painting was frivolous."

Diane's parents responded to her creativity with disapproval. She remembered vividly how her mother used to look upward and cry, "God, what did you send me?" referring to Diane. When Diane would draw or paint, her mother and aunt hid the paintings under the bed, telling her it was silly, she couldn't earn a living as an artist, and she should be more serious about her future.

It became clear that Diane's belief about not being good enough was a logical outcome of these experiences as a child. I helped her to see that there were other alternatives to explain the behavior of her parents and aunt.

"You formed the belief early on that you weren't good enough, based on the way you were treated," I observed. "It made sense to you. But now let's see if **I'm not good enough** was 'the truth' or if it was only your interpretation. Can you see other ways of explaining your mother's behavior toward you besides concluding that you weren't good enough?"

Diane nodded thoughtfully. "I don't know why, but I always assumed I deserved to be punished. It never occurred to me that I would be punished if I wasn't a bad person. But now, thinking about it, I realize my mother was a very unhappy woman, and she took her unhappiness out on me. I just assumed her harsh treatment of me was my fault, but that wasn't necessarily true."

"So another explanation for your mother's behavior was that she was unhappy and it had nothing to do with you. Can you think of other explanations?"

Diane came up with several:

1. It could mean that my family thought I wasn't good enough, but they were wrong.
2. Maybe I wasn't good enough by my family's standards, but I might be by the standards of other people.
3. In a Jewish family, painting is considered frivolous; in other environments it wouldn't be.
4. I wasn't good enough as a child; I might be fine when I grew up.

"I'll bet when you were a child you thought you could see your belief in the world, like a real, physical thing."

"Yes," she agreed. "It was as real as anything."

"But did you really see **I'm not good enough** in the world?"

"No, I didn't."

"If it wasn't 'out there,' then where was it?" I asked.

"I made it up. It was in my head."

"So do you still believe **I'm not good enough**?"

"No. It isn't true. It's gone."

This was a great revelation to Diane. Not only did she discover that the belief about herself wasn't "the truth" she also entered into a non-ordinary state of consciousness. She created herself as the creator of her life, and experienced nothing missing, endless possibilities, and no limitations.[6]

During the next four sessions, we continued to work on other related beliefs. Diane identified several: **I'm not worthy. I'm not capable. I'm warped. Nothing I can do is good enough. I'm alone in the world. I can't do what people expect of me.** Each of these beliefs, and others, were based on experiences that were similar to the childhood experiences she had described. As Diane began to eliminate them, one after the other, she was overwhelmed. "I realize now that none of these beliefs were the truth," she said. "I thought they were real, but they were just in my mind."

Now we were ready to go on.

Trapped in Life

During our fifth session together, we began to look at Diane's eating problem. She told me that she had tried every therapy, diet, book, and clinic she'd been able to find, and nothing helped.

"How would you describe your eating problem?" I asked. "Specifically, what is the dysfunctional pattern you've been trying unsuccessfully to change?"

She wasn't sure exactly what it was. She talked for about an hour, describing the present pattern and the events in her childhood that she felt were related to it.

"I don't think I reward myself with food, as I've been told," she said. "I see eating as a punishment. I don't ever get pleasure out of eating. What I eat is sweets and bread. I say, 'I don't want that, I don't even like that,' as I reach for a bagel or a piece of cake. I close the world off. I don't even hear the phone. I just eat."

She sighed. "I dream of being thin. I was skinny until my first child. I weighed ninety-two pounds at my wedding, when I was twenty-one. I've been fighting with my weight ever since."

It sounded as if Diane was making a connection between getting married and her weight problem. I sensed that there was another belief that needed to be eliminated before we could talk directly about her bulimia. I asked, "What did getting married and having children mean to you?"

"I don't think I ever wanted children." She paused, embarrassed. "I never said that to anyone before. I had my first child at twenty-three, and I never felt comfortable in the role of mother. My second child came when I was twenty-six. The way I see it, I succumbed. I became a housewife and mother. I hated to clean and couldn't cook. I gave up the art I loved. I was trapped, just like my mother was trapped."

"How was your mother trapped?"

"I used to catch her crying in the living room at night. A woman has no place to go. My mom and my aunts were all trapped. I said to myself, 'Once you have children, or are even just married, you're really stuck.' I decided very early that being married stinks.

As a kid I decided that the role of a woman is one of subservience, loss of identity, and loss of freedom. It's martyrdom. After my first child, what I feared came true. Early in my marriage, I resented having sex when my husband had the time and when *he* wanted it. I concluded that sex was up to one person. I'm alone a lot, and I eat when I'm alone. My husband and I live totally distinct and separate lives, even when we're together. We have for almost forty years."

Diane's eating pattern was not yet totally clear, but I asked her to try and identify a belief that might be responsible for the unhappiness that seemed to underlie it. She came up with this belief: **When a woman gets married and has children, she gives up herself and becomes totally subservient**.

Diane had already told me some of her childhood experiences that related to this belief, but she provided more details.

"Our lives were intertwined with Mom's five sisters. All six of them had terrible marriages. The men were very dominating, verbally and emotionally abusive. Only one of my aunts was dominant in her relationship with her husband. The men were tough adversaries. It looked like the only way to make it was to be a man."

After Diane listed several alternative explanations for her childhood experiences, I asked, "Do you remember being a child and seeing **When a woman gets married and has children, she gives up herself and becomes totally subservient**?"

"I do!" she replied instantly. "It was all around me, with my mother and my aunts."

"But did you really see it?"

"No, I didn't."

"What did you see?"

"I saw the women in my family getting married, having children, and giving up themselves."

"So your belief isn't '*the* truth.' You saw your mother and aunts being subservient, but is it clear to you now that your belief that all women become subservient was only one possible explanation for what you saw?"

Diane agreed, and the belief disappeared. Seeing that it was gone was a massive shock to her. Diane felt that her entire life had been based on the truth of this belief. She felt as if she had just eliminated the very foundation of her life. She was shaken.

We had started the session talking about food. Diane now saw that she started eating compulsively right after her first child, which led her to a belief that had to do with being married and having children.

We Tackle Bulimia

At the start of the next session, Diane was ready to tackle her pattern head-on.

We had a long conversation about eating. I asked her to think about when she ate, what she felt when she ate, and what she felt when she didn't eat. Her reflections took her back again to her childhood. She recalled several memories about food:

1. Mom was always on a diet because she had a bad stomach. She abused laxatives. Her sisters were the same.
2. When I was a child, my parents gave coffee and cake to guests.
3. Food and eating were part of our culture. Food was a gesture of welcome.
4. I liked sweets, and if I did something good, I'd get paid with sweets. If I was bad, I didn't get dessert. Being thin as a child was a form of rebellion.
5. As a kid, I associated meals with being attacked, with unpleasantness. Meals were 'let's get Diane' time. I hated to sit down at the table. I frequently threatened to vomit—and I *did* vomit if I was made to eat something I hated.

Diane went on to say, "They couldn't make me eat what I didn't want to eat. It was a way to assert personhood, my identity. Food makes me feel better, makes me feel warm. I get this wicked grin beating the system, getting my way. It's satisfaction—perverse satisfaction. I feel I'm my own person. I *will* be me."

She clearly remembered concluding at the age of three or four, **Eating is the only control I have over my life**.

When I asked her for some alternative interpretations of her childhood experiences, Diane had a hard time. This belief was so strongly "*the* truth" for her that she couldn't even imagine any alternatives. Eventually, however, she found several, and the belief disappeared.

Diane arrived at the next session and mentioned that she had seen significant changes in her life since we began our work. I read back to her every belief she had eliminated so far and asked her if any of them still seemed true for her. She shook her head and said no after each one.

But there was much more work to do.

Diane told me that she had eaten a lot one evening since our last session and had thrown it up. Earlier that evening she had hoped to speak to her husband, but he had gone to sleep before she could start a conversation. She went on to tell me how her marriage had evolved into such a lonely place for her.

"I always remembered how my father and uncle hated their jobs, and I didn't want that for my husband. I was very supportive when he took a night job so he could work days for himself. I wanted him to be able to do what he wanted to do. But that meant I was alone during the first nine years of my marriage. At first I didn't mind because I was excited about him starting his own business and being happy. But when my husband's business became successful and he gave up his evening work, he replaced it with evenings spent with clients. I could never get his attention. He even bragged that he had tunnel vision regarding his career. I couldn't be a part of his life. Business came first, second, third, and fourth. I might come fifth."

Suddenly, Diane began reflecting about her childhood observations of married life. It all came to the surface for her once again. "When I was a child, I saw that men were the bosses and women were subservient. Romantic relationships were not really romantic."

She stopped and stared at me with widened eyes. "That's it! That's the belief: **Marriage is the ruler and the slave. There's no truth, no honesty, no romance, no communication, no compassion.**"

"Great!" I said enthusiastically. Diane had just found a belief she had not been aware of previously. I reminded her that in earlier sessions she had clearly described several childhood events that could have led to that conclusion. She recalled them briefly and was able to create a series of alternative explanations.

After the belief disappeared, Diane could imagine all sorts of possibilities in her relationship with her husband that she hadn't been able to imagine before. She wasn't sure what to do and how to do it, but she left excited.

What had occurred was the discovery that one stimulus to eating was her loneliness and being ignored by her husband. So we eliminated a core belief that had led to her loneliness.

At the next session, Diane described her eating pattern as she then saw it. "I'm eating when I have negative feelings. I feel I should not have negative feelings. When I have so much [materially], I shouldn't have negative feelings. Even as a child I had everything I needed. I certainly do now. What right do I have to be depressed or upset? When I feel really upset, I eat to numb myself so I don't feel. When I eat to numb out, I'm gone."

She identified two survival strategy beliefs: **Eating is the only way to cover the pain** and **Food is my only way to produce pleasure and love.**

As she reviewed the events of her childhood, Diane said, "I used not-eating as a weapon against my mother. She believed food was love. Cookies and candy were a reward for being good, and when she gave them to me I felt loved—something I rarely felt. Then, after my first child was born and I was miserable, I ate and the pain diminished. I had discovered—actually, I had created—a connection between food and emotions."

After Diane had found other alternatives for her childhood experiences and the two beliefs disappeared, she began for the first time to really grasp that she could change her eating pattern.

Diane Looks Deeper

When we met again, Diane reported, "A lot of things are changing, but food is still tough. I still run to the refrigerator when

I'm alone, although I'm much more aware of what I'm doing now. I can't close my head off the way I used to. I talk to myself now: 'Do you need it? No, I want it.' I threw up once last week after eating two boxes of cookies. I knew I'd 'give it back' when I ate them. I still feel as if I have no control at the moment. When I ate the cookies I felt, *screw you*. I know I shouldn't do this and I will anyway.

"I can't stand the feeling of having food in me, and yet I go to the refrigerator two hundred times a day. The action of eating is pleasant but always tinged with guilt. It's pure relief to get rid of it. I feel relief, calm, release."

Diane began to reflect on what was behind this experience of relief, calm, and release. She recalled, "About twenty years ago I came home after a dinner with my husband and a client and threw up because I was so stuffed. And that started the binge-and-purge syndrome. I merely observed one day that when I overate I felt I was punished by the vomiting, so I consciously decided to overeat in order to punish myself. It's complicated, because after vomiting I also feel calm and good."

The belief was obvious: **The only way to achieve release and calm is to vomit—to give it back**. A related belief was **Vomiting is a way to control my life**.

This was an interesting session because the two beliefs had been formed years before they produced the pattern. We had started by looking at her statement that the only way to survive as a child was to "give it back" when she was forced to eat something she didn't want to eat. Later in life it looked as if she was throwing up primarily when she felt guilty, upset, depressed, and out of control. I got the sense that part of her reason for eating was to have something to throw up. The eating problem had started at twenty-three when her first child was born. The vomiting hadn't started for another twenty years.

I suggested to Diane, and she agreed, that the first time she threw up as an adult was not to assert control, feel calm, and experience a release (which was the childhood belief). Rather, it was an accident because she had felt so stuffed after dinner. Afterward, however, she noticed that she did experience a psychological release, a calm and control that was consistent with the childhood decision. That experience reminded her of the childhood belief. She experienced the same good feelings after accidentally throwing up. Thereafter, she consciously decided to adopt that behavior in order to produce the feelings that accompanied the vomiting.

At her next session Diane reported that her eating was very different. "I don't feel as panicky about food. I had some dessert last week. I rarely only have 'some.' Normally the thought of food is in the forefront of my mind. Now, however, I feel I can stop. I can push a plate away. I couldn't before. I am seeing major changes in my eating patterns."

"My Best Friend"

The next time we met, Diane made an interesting comment. She said she was feeling less compulsive in her eating, calmer and more centered. Now the issue was, "I don't want to give up my best friend"—meaning food.

"What is the belief underneath that?"

"I guess that **Food is my best friend**," Diane said shyly. "It's my comfort; it's the only thing that's always there when I need it.

"When I was alone in my twenties, when I had no control over my life, I had an enormous responsibility as a wife, mother, partner, and housewife. I wasn't prepared for it. I didn't know how to cook or be my husband's 'business partner.' I was scared to death. I sewed, painted, and ate. I always felt better when I ate."

As she was looking for the source of the belief **Food is my best friend**, she discovered another one: **Eating is a way to hide, something to hide behind**.

When the initial belief disappeared, this second one did too, without working on it specifically. She then mentioned that she was upset because she couldn't seem to hold on to the experience of being the creator of her life between sessions.

I explained, "No one can hold on to it. It can't be remembered; it has to be created anew." I reminded her about the three ways of knowing: understanding, experiencing, and creating. She claimed that she *understood* that she was the creator of her life between sessions, and she experienced it from time to time, but she only *created* it as true when she did the LBP with me.

I reminded Diane that she had told me in a recent session that she did have the internal sense between sessions of experiencing herself as the source of her beliefs, rather than as merely her body and beliefs. She remembered that conversation and acknowledged that the experience was becoming more real for her between sessions. TLM was working.

That was the last time I saw Diane for a while, because she was traveling with her husband. We finally had a telephone session about a month later. It seemed that the major remaining issue was her relationship with her husband. Not being "seen" by him was the one thing that still upset her, and she couldn't deal with it. Eating was still her survival strategy. Thus, when she announced early in the conversation that she had gone back to eating whole desserts, bread and butter, and more, I was disappointed but not surprised.

"I'm uncomfortable in my skin," she said. "And I'm uncomfortable with my husband. He cares more about the people at work and his friends than he does about me. He won't take me seriously. I'm very upset about it. I want companionship, communication with my husband."

Diane also revealed another thing that was troubling her, something that was a result of our working together.

"I've been changing over the past few months and he hasn't. I want him to change, and he isn't even making an attempt. Before this work on my beliefs, I didn't even see the possibility that our relationship could be any different. Now I can see the possibility, but I can't have it." She laughed bitterly. "What a dilemma! And it's so painful to be with him. It's easier to eat bread and butter than to talk to him."

"So you're not pursuing the new possibilities that have opened up for you?" I asked.

"I'm afraid of rocking the boat, of being alone," she admitted. "And I can't stand having the failure of not being able to make the marriage work. I've paid an awful price for comfort and don't want to give that up. I'm also, frankly, afraid I'll never find anyone else. I've always looked down on someone who's gotten divorced. It would mean that everyone would see my failure. Shame. Fear. I couldn't make a go of it."

"So what is the belief?" I prodded gently.

"It's a woman's responsibility to make a marriage work. If she doesn't, there's something wrong with her."

That belief clearly explained Diane's guilt about not being able to make her marriage work and her unwillingness to even consider divorce. I was careful to emphasize that I wasn't recommending divorce, but I urged her to eliminate the belief that made divorce impossible, so she could choose to stay rather than *have* to stay because of the belief.

She thought about the source of the belief. "I guess it's that my family always said, '*She* couldn't make it work,' whenever a couple we knew got divorced. Very few women got divorced at the time; it was the shame of the century. It was always the woman's fault they couldn't make it work, no matter how mean or miserable the man was. None of my mother's sisters had a good marriage, yet none ever got a divorce."

Again, the belief disappeared after Diane made up several alternatives and realized she never saw the belief in the world. I was very pleased with the progress we were making. Diane had already eliminated quite a few beliefs.

Diane Disappears

Then Diane disappeared. I called and left several messages over the next few months, but she didn't return any of my calls. I wrote, and the letter went unanswered. I called again several months later, and still no reply. I had an idea about why she totally cut off all communication, but there was no way to know for sure. Based on the work we had been doing when she stopped, it looked as if Diane was afraid to look any deeper into her relationship with her husband. She didn't even want to consider the possibility that she could leave him. That would have been too scary for her.

I decided that if she didn't want to talk, for whatever reason, I had to honor that decision. And there it remained for eighteen months, at which point I started working on this book. I wanted to use Diane as a case history, so I read through her file. When I finished, I had to know how she was.

I called, and her husband answered. When he asked who was calling, I answered, "It's Morty." *Oh, shoot*, I thought; if only she had answered the phone herself. Now she'd have him make an excuse for her. But a moment later I heard her voice.

"It's good to hear from you."

I told her I had been reading through her file and thinking about her. "How have you been?"

"I'd like to talk." she said warmly. "But I'm about to go out right now. Call me tomorrow and we'll set a time to get together." I called the next day and we agreed to meet a few weeks later.

Diane breezed into my office, looking wonderful and happier than I'd ever seen her. She plunked herself down on the sofa and started talking. "I had lost myself; now I'm finding myself," she said proudly. "So many things have happened. One is that my husband's been sick. He's frightened, and that's opened the door to us talking. He's begun to hear me. I wanted him to know I would no longer be the person I had been, and it was okay for him to be the way he is. That really shook him up. I wanted my freedom, but I didn't know that I had it all along. I just had to take it.

"My husband will never change. And that's really okay with me. It used to be when he came home upset, I'd say, 'What can I do to make it better?' Now I say, 'I'm sorry you had such a bad day. Is there something I can do to help you relax?' I do what I can to help, but it's no longer up to me to make it all better. I'm far more relaxed with him. He doesn't intimidate me the way he used to. I don't feel inadequate anymore, even if a painting—I've been painting again—isn't perfect."

I asked Diane about her eating. "I've been pretty good about it," she said. "I'm working with a holistic doctor to create a fat-free diet. I can now turn away from desserts, but bread is still difficult. So I bake my own fat-free bread."

"What about binging and purging?" I asked.

"Only three times since I saw you eighteen months ago. I used to do it three times a day. If I hadn't found a way to stop, I'd be dead by now. The three instances were times when I felt overwhelming hopelessness. My need to be who I want to be for myself was being stepped on. I used to attribute that feeling to my husband's not being what I wanted him to be. Not so. I now see it has nothing to do with anyone but me. I no longer have the need to vomit."

I read back the list of beliefs Diane had eliminated during our sessions. There were almost thirty of them.[2]

"Gone," she said with a dazzling smile after each one.

"Tell me how you've seen changes in your patterns as a result," I said.

"I now experience freedom without guilt," she said. "It's okay for me to not sit home and wait for my husband to show up. For example, we bought tickets to a show a few weeks ago. At the last minute he called and said he wasn't going to be able to make it. In the past I would have called someone and given the two tickets away and stayed home. This time I called someone and said I had one extra ticket, not two and asked her to come with me. We had a great dinner and then enjoyed the show. It's now okay for me to enjoy myself."

She talked and talked about her new sense of freedom. She no longer felt she was responsible for everyone else's happiness. She was doing what she wanted to do for herself. She was not being nasty to others, but she was also not allowing them to impinge on her newly created sense of freedom.

At some point I stopped her and asked, "What happened eighteen months ago? Why wouldn't you talk to me?"

Her face reddened. "I'm embarrassed about that," she said. "But it was too scary. If I took the next step, what would I land on?"

Diane had been scared of all the possibilities she'd created for herself. She wasn't sure of her footing. She had floundered for a few months, but as she got more comfortable with the numerous possibilities that arose after the beliefs disappeared, she started creating a brand-new life for herself, a life in which food was no longer an issue and in which she was now free to be herself.

At the end of the session, she smiled and hugged me. I remembered that she had said to me several times during our meetings that she was sorry she hadn't discovered TLM earlier in her life. I always answered, "It's never too late to create your life. You're in your early sixties. You probably have another twenty years that you can live as the creator of your life." She always nodded that she understood what I was saying, but I could tell that the regret about the past had seemed more real to her than the opportunity for the future. Now, as she walked away, I realized that she had finally put aside the past and was creating her future just the way she wanted it.

I called Diane again about a year later. We chatted for a few minutes about her life during the prior year. I could hear the happiness and excitement in her voice as she described a number of positive changes, including the fact that she hadn't had a single bulimic incident. She summed everything up by concluding, "You just can't believe how good it is on this end of the phone."

Chapter 7

Case History Barry: A Transformed Criminal

I'm thinking of the people who won't get shot in the future because I just got rid of these beliefs.
—Barry

As you saw in the last case study, TLM has the power to permanently transform lives. I've seen it happen hundreds of times. You may, however, like many others, also believe that there are some individuals who are "hopeless."

I was eager to demonstrate that TLM could be effective with men who were used to being judged by others as incapable of change and simply not worth the effort.

In 1994, I decided to conduct a small pilot study that would involve sixteen incarcerated young men, eight of whom would be part of a control group and eight of whom I would have a weekly LBP session with for three months. I knew many people would look at these men and doubt that they could change. There is a common idea that there is nothing we can do about crime except lock the criminals up and throw away the key. Given most of the evidence thus far, especially the high rate of recidivism, this belief makes a lot of sense.

I wanted to demonstrate a new possibility. I began looking for subjects and for a psychologist to actually design the parameters of the study. I called Professor of Psychology Lee Sechrest at the University of Arizona, who had written about research methods in the *Handbook of Juvenile Delinquency*. He agreed to choose the measures and analyze the data.[1]

Early in August, I met with teenagers at Long Lane School, an institution for incarcerated teenagers, and with adults at Maple

Street House, a halfway house where convicts went after release from prison but before being totally freed.

I spoke frankly with them. "I've never been arrested," I said, "but when I was a kid I had a lot of problems, and I was depressed for much of my life." I described how nothing I had done, including therapy, had made much difference for me. But when I discovered that my problems were all the result of my beliefs, and when I eliminated the appropriate beliefs, my life improved dramatically. I asked them if they would like to be part of a research study to determine if eliminating beliefs could be helpful to people who had been arrested for criminal behavior. Most of those I talked to volunteered to participate, and we had our sixteen subjects.

The pilot study proved to be a great success. It provided statistical evidence to buttress anecdotal stories from hundreds of case histories that showed behavior is the result of specific beliefs, that the beliefs can be eliminated, and that the behavior will change when the beliefs disappear. I now had scientific evidence that it's not the environment that produces criminal behavior, it's the beliefs formed in the environment.

Once again, it is not what happens to you during your childhood that affects you- it is what you conclude about what happens to you—your beliefs—that determine the rest of your life.

After analyzing the results of the study, Dr. Sechrest wrote, "The simplest and, we think, fairly compelling conclusion is that the intervention [TLM] resulted in generally favorable changes in self-concept in the experimental group and that, without intervention, self-concepts would likely have deteriorated during confinement."

After analyzing the data from the two measures filled out by subjects and the one completed by counselors, Dr. Sechrest concluded:

> The results strongly support the claim that persons in the experimental condition did develop more favorable self-concepts over the weeks of the experiment, while those in the control condition showed no systematic change. . . .

Similarly, by self-reports, the persons in the experimental group also improved more in several behavioral dispositions likely to be related to risk of further legal violations. Specifically, the experimental group improved more (statistically significant) than the controls on the Inwald, a test aimed at detecting social deviance. The experiments also showed statistically significant improvements on risk-taking tendencies and leadership.... All in all, this little experiment has to be regarded as a fairly remarkable success. Certainly it justifies efforts to carry out further testing to determine whether the changes observed can be dependably produced. If they can, TLM could have definite promise in helping young male offenders mend their ways.

My conviction that TLM would work as well with a criminal population had been justified. Conducting the study was also a deeply moving and transforming experience for me. Barry's story is a case in point.

Barry—In the Beginning

Barry was a tall, thin, twenty-two-year-old African American. He looked very serious and rarely smiled. He had been arrested for larceny third, which he described as driving a stolen car and possessing a gun. Barry had served his time in prison and was at Maple Street House when I met him. When our sessions began, he was looking for a job but hadn't found one yet. In spite of his problems with the law, Barry was extremely bright and motivated. He didn't want to set foot in prison ever again.

I worked with Barry two hours a week for thirteen weeks—the period we were confined to by the study. Normally, TLM would be more open-ended, because there's no way to know at the beginning how many beliefs need eliminating. Even with our limited time, however, much was accomplished. In thirteen weeks, Barry eliminated thirty-two beliefs—as well as several criminal and other dysfunctional behavior patterns.

The following case history details some of the most critical breakthroughs that came during Barry's LBP sessions. It will give you an idea of what is possible—even for a young man like Barry whom society had in so many ways abandoned.

There is, of course, more to Barry's story than you will see here. The following story is significantly abridged. More beliefs and patterns were eliminated than are described here. But you *will* see how the steps of the LBP can stop criminal behavior and change a violent lifestyle. If TLM can change patterns so extreme, imagine what it can do for you.

At our first session, I reviewed what I had told Barry and the others about TLM at our initial meeting. He listened quietly, his usual serious expression on his face. I think he was probably wondering what he'd gotten himself into.

"What I need from you," I said, "is some pattern of behavior or feelings that you have tried unsuccessfully to change."

Barry took what seemed like an eternity to answer.

"I'm not very good with people," he said finally. "I stay quiet and don't talk in groups. I feel upset, jumpy. I worry about what they'll think about what I say. I feel they'll be against me."

Despite his long pauses, it didn't take much time for Barry to find a belief that could explain his pattern: **I'm not worthwhile**.

"Where did that belief come from?" I asked. "What happened early in your life that could have led to that conclusion?"

Barry began to tell me the story of his troubled childhood. "I had a sister, one year older than me, and two brothers, two and four years older. My father had a full-time job working as a machinist. But he left when I was four for about six years to live with another woman. He eventually had thirteen children, with a lot of different women. What I remember about him is that he was an alcoholic. Loud. He didn't hit me, though. He didn't do much of anything with me when I was little. We had no relationship before he left. He didn't even say much to me. He did yell at me if I didn't do my chores. I was always scared of him, drunk or sober. He always carried a gun. He had shot people.

"My mother worked as a nurse. She was quiet, very quiet. She got upset if we didn't do what we were told. She'd spank me and say, 'I work all the time, why don't you do what I ask?' Most of the time she was warm and loving, but she wasn't around very much.

"We were raised by an aunt who was very loud and always criticizing us. She'd yell and curse at us if we were too noisy, if we left our toys out, if we didn't clean our rooms. She'd always be saying, 'Your asses are lazy.' She'd spank us with a belt."

Barry acknowledged that the way his three caregivers had treated him led to the belief **I'm not worthwhile**. I helped him to find several alternative interpretations for the events of his childhood and to realize that he had never seen his beliefs in the world—they were just his interpretation of events. After going through the remaining steps of the LBP, the belief **I'm not worthwhile** was gone. He was beginning to experience a new possibility—that he could eliminate his dysfunctional beliefs.

How Barry Survived

At our next session I reviewed the pattern from the first session, and Barry identified another belief that contributed to it: **I'm not good enough**. I asked him what he experienced in childhood that led to this conclusion.

In addition to the childhood events he had described earlier, Barry recalled, "Nobody noticed what I did. Nobody noticed me. If I got a good grade in school, no one cared."

"Do you remember any physical, emotional, or verbal demonstrativeness toward you by your family?" I asked.

"No. There was none."

"Okay, so as a result of not being noticed or shown affection, you concluded **I'm not good enough**."

"Right." Barry nodded.

We went through the remaining steps of the LBP, and Barry's belief **I'm not good enough** disappeared. Then I explained to Barry about survival strategy beliefs. "What did you use to make yourself feel worthwhile and good enough?" I asked.

"The more people who spoke to me and respected me, the better I'd feel," Barry said. He came up with the survival strategy belief **The way to be good enough is to have people interested in you**.

He was clear about the source of this belief. "My sister did favors for everybody. She'd go to the store, wash dishes, and help people. She got rewards: money and attention. She got attention all the time, compared to the boys. She got to go everywhere with Mom: shopping, visiting—wherever Mom went. The family was more interested in her. They showed that by buying her clothes, taking her places, spending more time with her, not yelling at her, not spanking her. It was clear that she was better than me."

At our third session, Barry reported, "I've been speaking up more lately and I'm not as concerned about other people. I'm still pretty quiet, though."

Even though there had been a change in the pattern, it had not disappeared totally, which meant there were other beliefs to be identified and eliminated. He found more: **People can't be trusted. People are dishonest**.

"As a kid if I made a comment about someone, another kid would tell him. If I told girls what I felt, they'd tell other kids who'd make fun of me. I liked sitting in the dark, watching stars. People made fun of that, too.

"I used to depend a lot on my brother who was closest in age to me. He used to promise that I could ride his bike and wear his shirt. There were a lot of things he said he would do for me that were important to me. He never came through for me."

After discovering alternative interpretations and completing the steps of the LBP, these beliefs, too, disappeared.

Barry started our fourth session by telling me, "I speak up now. I don't think about what other people think of me. All the beliefs we talked about are gone. My pattern is different."

"What pattern do you want to work on now?" I asked.

"Violence. Since I was fifteen I've shot three people and shot at others when I get angry." Barry confessed. "Last night I gave my waitress twenty dollars and she gave me change for a five. The manager came over and quickly checked the register and said I had given her five dollars. He was calling me a liar. I started swearing at them and threatening them. I got my money. I was thinking about getting my gun and going back. I'm usually patient, but when I get mad, I want to shoot people."

As we discussed the pattern as it had existed throughout his life, Barry realized that every time he shot someone or felt like shooting someone, "I felt disrespected. I got angry and wanted to shoot them to stop the disrespect."

I explained that we were looking for survival strategy beliefs. "You don't feel good enough or worthwhile. When you think people are disrespecting you, you are brought face-to-face with those beliefs, which produces a lot of anxiety. Using a gun is your way to stop them from reminding you that you aren't good enough or worthwhile. What are the specific words of your belief?"

"My survival strategy is my pride. I can't survive without that. If I don't get respect, I'll look bad, I'll feel stupid, I'll feel bad about myself. **The way to feel important is to be respected. The way to be respected is to use a gun.**"

Barry told me about his father. "He took me to clubs when I was a kid. People respected him, ran up to him, knew his name. He seemed important. He always told me, 'Let people know you're not going to take any shit and you'll be respected.' Also, in the street, the people who were respected were the ones who carried and used guns."

"So you drew the logical conclusion that carrying a gun would get you respect," I said.

He nodded.

"Barry, can you see that your conclusion wasn't wrong? In fact, it made a lot of sense, based on what you observed as a child."

I asked Barry to think of alternative explanations for his belief. He came up with:

1. The way my father was respected was to use a gun. It might not work for other people.
2. The way to be respected in my old neighborhood was to use a gun. It might not work in other places.
3. One way to be respected is to use a gun, but it has a lot of negative consequences. There might be other ways to be respected that don't carry the negative consequences.

"Didn't it seem as a kid that you could see with your eyes that **The way to be respected is to use a gun**?" I asked.

"Oh, yes," Barry replied.

"Look again. Did you really see that in the world?"

"I guess not. No. I didn't."

"Now," I asked, "do you believe it's the truth that **The way to be respected is to use a gun**?"

"No, I don't," Barry said, with a surprised look on his face.

"So you've just eliminated that belief."

Barry grinned. "Yes, I guess I have."

At the next session he reported two incidents that showed him that the patterns were changing. "I had been talking on the phone when a girl said to me, 'I can't stand you.' Normally I would have started swearing. But this time, I just ignored it and went on talking on the phone. Also, I deliberately spent some time with my old buddies over the weekend. They were carrying their guns. I felt like going home to get mine, but instead I just left it. I had wanted to see how I would feel and what I would do."

I suggested that we look for other beliefs involving guns because, although he had left his buddies over the weekend, he had still felt like getting his gun. Barry came up with the beliefs **I'm not important** and **I'm alone in the world** and the survival strategy belief: **The way to be important is to hang out with the popular crowd and do what they're doing**.

In addition to everything Barry had already told me about his childhood, he added a few more details to account for the beliefs **I'm not important** and **I'm alone in the world**. "My aunt was always saying, 'Don't bug me!' My mom worked all day and wasn't around, and she was too tired to be with me when she got home. She didn't buy me the things that my friends' parents did."

The two beliefs disappeared after he created several alternative explanations for the events in his childhood, and after he realized that he never saw the beliefs in the world.

"Tell me about your survival strategy belief **The way to be important is to hang out with the popular crowd and do what they're doing**," I said.

Barry told me he'd always hung out with people who carried guns. "They get a lot of attention from the people in the neighborhood. When you're one of them you get a lot of attention too. It makes you important."

We had found another survival strategy belief involving guns. It was becoming clear to me from my work with Barry and the other incarcerated subjects that they had the same negative self-esteem beliefs that I and most of my noncriminal clients had. The difference between us was not in the level of self-esteem. It was in the survival strategy beliefs that the subjects had chosen, to deal with or compensate for their low self-esteem, compared to those chosen by noncriminals. As always, the source of the beliefs was the immediate environment.

In most law-abiding, middle-class families, children get attention, respect, and love when they get good grades or do what their parents say, and they notice that the people around them who get attention, respect, and love are successful in the professional or business world. On the other hand, people who end up as criminals get attention, respect, and love from others in their community when they get into trouble, and they notice that the people around them who get attention, respect, and love are gang members and people who carry guns, break the law, are violent, and sell drugs.

"I used to try to hang out with the crowd my brother hung out with, but they said I was too young," Barry said. "My brother was popular in that crowd, with girls too. I found other kids who were popular; they were the tough guys—always fighting, breaking windows, and getting into trouble. I wanted to be known. The kids in the gangs wore jackets; they were popular. I wanted to be part of it."

After the beliefs were eliminated, I said to Barry, "Now, step back. Can you imagine the possibility of hanging out with people who have guns but not carrying one yourself anymore because you don't need it to be important?"

He nodded silently. In that moment he fully experienced himself as the creator of his life. He was clear that everything in his life was a function of his beliefs.

"You know," he said in a soft voice just before the session ended, "I never told you before, but I have two little kids: a son one-and-a-half years old and a daughter four months. They have different mothers, and I didn't marry them. But I want to be a better father to them than mine was."

Barry Faces His Anger

Barry arrived at our next session, smiling a rare smile and seeming very pleased with himself. He reported that he had just gotten a job entering data in computers for a *Fortune* 500 company. Barry wanted to do well at his job and eliminate all of his dysfunctional patterns. He proudly informed me, "I don't need a gun anymore."

We picked up where the last session had ended—with his dysfunctional relationships with women.

"I've been in a lot of shaky relationships," Barry said. "They don't last long. There's lots of arguments, especially about cheating."

I helped Barry identify some beliefs that were producing this pattern. He came up with: **Women are unfaithful. Relationships are trouble. Women are distrustful of men.** The source of the first two beliefs was his first two relationships, when he and the girls were fourteen or fifteen years old. "Both of them cheated on me. When I confronted them with what I knew, they denied it. I checked it out and found out it was true. We argued about it and I finally beat them up. The relationships ended. When I saw them later, they said nasty things to me and said bad things about me to other girls I was going with."

The source of the third belief was his mother, who always told him, "Men are whores. Men are liars. Men are sneaky." His aunt and female cousins frequently said the same thing.

Barry's survival strategy was again to use violence. He beat up his girlfriends, and he admitted to beating up other women too.

"When I feel mad I can't deal with being mad. I just lash out," Barry said. "The purpose is to punish the person for doing something that made me mad. When what they did that made me mad stays in my mind, my only thought is, 'I'm going to hurt them.' What makes me mad is someone disrespecting me."

I asked, "What beliefs would you have to have to explain that behavior?" Barry came up with three beliefs: **I don't matter. People who make you feel bad should be punished. The way to punish people is to make them feel pain.**

The source of the first belief was the same family events that produced **I'm not good enough.** The source of the other two beliefs was very simple: "When I upset my family, they beat me." (So much for the theory that corporal punishment is a good way to discipline children!)

After these three beliefs were gone, Barry was quiet for a long time. I didn't say anything because he seemed to be deep in thought. Finally, I asked him what he was thinking. His answer stunned me.

"I'm thinking of the people who won't get shot in the future because I just got rid of these beliefs. And I'm thinking of the people who got shot in the past because I had these beliefs. I once shot up someone real bad for five dollars. I could have talked to him and collected a dollar a week. I once shot a guy because he said to my girl, 'Come here.' I thought he was disrespecting me. You've got to get this [TLM] to the kids before it's too late. Before they kill someone and it's too late. I'll talk to them with you."

I had done TLM with a lot of clients who had made many major changes in their lives before this session, but rarely had I been so moved and inspired. If I ever had any reservations about the efficacy of TLM in alleviating crime and violence, they were totally gone now.

Barry showed up for the next session looking lighter, more relaxed. I asked him what changes he was noticing in his life.

"I'm more positive. If someone says something that normally would have upset me, I tend to ignore it and not get mad," he replied. "That's a big deal for me. I just *feel* better, you know?"

Barry had mentioned in an earlier session that he had two young children. Each child had a different mother, and Barry hadn't married either of them. I reminded him of this and suggested we use it as a pattern. "What do you believe," I asked, "that could account for this situation?"

As usual, Barry didn't have much trouble coming up with a belief: **The way to keep women around without being committed to them is to have children with them**.

He also had no trouble finding the source of the belief. "My father had thirteen children with five different women. He used to take me to different houses to visit the kids. I saw he wasn't committed to any of the mothers. None of them were with another man, either. My father would visit the kids and then spend the night with the mother."

We spent some time thinking of alternatives to the belief Barry had formed after observing his father's behavior, and the belief disappeared. It was no longer "the truth" for Barry.

After the belief disappeared, Barry said solemnly, "If I hadn't had this belief, I never would have had my daughter."

We still had plenty of time, so I asked him, "What do you believe about how to get what you want?"

He identified two beliefs: **To get what I want is impossible. The way to get what I want is to take it from whoever has it.**

The source of the first belief was never getting what he wanted as a kid. It seemed to Barry that no one cared about how he felt, what he did, what he thought, or what he wanted. The second belief was a survival strategy Barry created after he formed the first belief. Its source was noticing that all the guys in his neighborhood took whatever they wanted. When they wanted food, clothes, bikes, or anything else, they simply grabbed them from stores or from other people.

Barry Finds Hope

At our next session, I decided to try something I had done with a few clients in the past. "Barry," I said, "instead of starting with a pattern and then looking for a belief, I'd like you to look inside yourself and find your sense of life. This exists as a feeling, as a sense, not as words. It is your deepest sense of yourself. After you have found the feeling, you can describe it in words, but it exists in you as a feeling, not as a concept."

He thought for a few minutes and then spoke: "Life's a struggle; you have to strive for what you want; it doesn't come easy; things are complicated, hard to understand."

He paused for a minute and then continued. "As a kid, that's all I saw—people struggling. There wasn't enough money to pay bills, to buy food, to pay for the car. I didn't understand what I was seeing, and no one explained it to me. Mom had to go to work and school and be away, and I didn't understand that."

Barry then reviewed some of the events from his childhood that he had told me at earlier sessions. When he was clear that he knew the source of his sense of life, he found alternative explanations. When we were done, that deep emotional sense of life he had lived with since childhood was gone.

As I drove away I was thinking, "Here's a guy with nothing more than a high school education, who recently was out on the street shooting people, who now is clear that he creates his own reality, that he creates all meaning, that his entire life is a function of his beliefs—which he can change at any time. If a few LBP sessions could lead Barry to taking responsibility for his life, the implications are staggering! What if I could train tens of thousands of people to use TLM with millions of kids, both in and out of prison?"

Barry walked into his next session talking. "I'm feeling more control. I'm not letting my temper run me as much. The other night someone took a few bucks out of my wallet, and I didn't even get mad. A few months ago, I would have threatened everyone in the room. I'm getting a sense, even between sessions, of being the creator. I talk to myself, like, 'I can do *this*. I don't have to do *that*.' I saw this group of guys carrying guns and I thought, I don't need to do that. I have nothing to prove."

He was smiling throughout his entire report. A transformation had taken place before my eyes.

The next issue to handle was Barry's return to society. We discussed the artificial, restricted environment in which he was living—an environment that didn't expose him to much of life.

Thus, a lot of dysfunctional patterns that might exist out in the "real world" were not arising while he was living in a halfway house.

We decided to look at potential problems that might arise when he was released. "What about a career?" I asked.

"I want to be an accountant. I took high school courses and business school courses in accounting. I like working with numbers. I liked math in school. I want to go to college and become a CPA. I'm working for a company now that would pay part of my tuition. I haven't really thought much about it. I'll be out of here [Maple Street House] in about two months."

"What do you believe could prevent you from becoming a CPA?"

He identified three patterns and their accompanying beliefs. The first concern he had was that he might not have enough money to pay for college. The belief was **Money is tight**.

"As a kid, Mom never had enough money to do what she wanted to do. She was always telling me I couldn't have what I wanted because there wasn't enough money."

The second issue was "It might interfere with my social life. I might miss out on fun if I study all the time. I might lose all my women. It's an image thing." The belief associated with that feeling was **What makes me feel attractive is having a lot of women interested in me**. Barry told me the source of that belief. "When I was about eleven or twelve years old and my brother's girlfriend, who was sixteen or seventeen, came around, she said, 'You're so cute,' which made me feel attractive. If she thought I was attractive, it meant I was. I also remember a group of girls got together and decided which one of them would talk to me, and I knew that. That also made me feel attractive, knowing they were all interested in me."

Both beliefs were eliminated during this session. Barry found a survival strategy belief associated with the second belief: **In order to feel good about myself, I need to be attractive**. He recalled, "As an early teenager my friends had new clothes, and I didn't. They got a lot of attention, and I didn't. I felt bad, left out, depressed. When I got new clothes, I got attention; I wasn't left out,

I felt happy, good. As a teen I only felt good when getting attention, which I got mainly from wearing new clothes. I remember when I was about fourteen, hanging out with a cousin who was about eighteen. He always had new clothes and looked nice. He was always telling me to 'look good.' So when I put on nice clothes I felt good. He took me to sporting events and concerts and he had me dress up when we went. He took me shopping for clothes and told me how good I looked when I was dressed up. He told me what to wear, what I looked good in. I respected him a lot."

The next aspect of the going-to-college pattern was his fear that "I won't apply myself. I'm afraid to fail." The belief responsible for that feeling was **I don't have the ability to get through college to be a CPA.** Its source was the fact that only a few of his friends had gone to college, and some of them had flunked out. We went through the LBP and Barry saw that his belief wasn't "the truth."

After he had eliminated all the beliefs we could find that might have prevented him from becoming a CPA, I asked him to imagine the entire process of applying for school, getting money from his present employer to help pay for tuition, finding other sources of tuition funds, getting accepted, going to school, studying, and being busy evenings with little time for dating. Then I asked him to see if he experienced any concerns or problems at any step along the way. After thinking for three or four minutes, he looked straight at me and said, "I can see it happen now. . . now that I've gotten rid of these beliefs. I'll be a CPA."

At my last session with Barry, I went back and reviewed all the patterns involving violence and guns. Then I asked him, "Can you imagine any possible situation that would lead you to use a gun or engage in any other form of violence?"

He thought for a minute or so. "If someone deliberately stood in my face and degraded me—you know, called me a punk— I still feel I have to shoot him. All the other things I mentioned before wouldn't bother me, but this one thing would."

"What belief would produce that reaction?"

Barry said immediately, "**Allowing someone to stand in my face and talk junk to me means I'm not a man.**"

"Do you really believe that statement?" I asked quietly.

"Yes!" His answer was firm.

"Tell me, Barry, does some part of you also know that you made it up, that it is really '*a* truth' not '*the* truth'?"

He smiled sheepishly and nodded. It was clear that Barry was in the space of the creator, even though he had beliefs that hadn't yet been eliminated which could cause him problems in his life.

He found the source of this belief. "My father used to tell me that. He took me to these clubs with him, and when someone didn't stand up for himself, my father would tell me the person was a punk—he wasn't a man. My father told me never to do that."

After Barry looked at several alternative interpretations and realized he had never seen his belief in the world, I asked, "It isn't 'the truth,' is it?

"No, it isn't," Barry said. "It isn't 'the truth' and I don't believe it."

Making a Difference

Barry had many obstacles to overcome and many beliefs to eliminate. Even though he had eliminated thirty-two beliefs by the time we ended our work together, I would have liked to have had more time with Barry. It just wasn't possible to discover and eliminate every belief responsible for all his dysfunctional patterns in so short a time.[2]

Even so, Barry and I completed our thirteen sessions with high hopes. At the end of our final session, Barry looked at me shyly and said, "Just possibly, I want to try to help the younger kids growing up now. You know, the ones hanging out on the streets. Try to be a role model, you know? I could preach to them about the stuff I went through while I was out running in the streets. Try to show them a different way—a positive way. So, you know, I want to try and do something like that. Sort of like giving back to the community. I know kids now, eight and nine years old, they're lost out there. I'd tell them, 'You don't have to do this. You don't have to think that selling drugs or whatever is going to make you some big person. There's something else.'"

Shortly after the study ended, I was describing what happened to a law enforcement official. "It sounds like you're just telling these guys 'You're not responsible for what you did because of your beliefs and childhood experiences,'" he said. "Isn't it just another variation on blaming your parents or someone else?"

I realized that this was the way some people might interpret the work. Yet TLM is all about taking responsibility! That's what being the creator means. My friend's observation was correct in the sense that a person's range of responses is limited when he experiences himself as the creation. But the goal of TLM is to assist people to live as the creator and thus to take the ultimate responsibility. We have less power in the short term (as the creation) and more power ultimately (as the creator) than we usually assume.

A Serious Vision of Rehabilitation

Despite the excellent results of my work with Barry and the others in the study, I know that merely offering TLM to incarcerated criminals is not the answer to the problem of violence and crime. If used with convicted criminals and people exhibiting criminal behavior who have not been arrested, TLM can make a tremendous impact both in prevention and rehabilitation, because it can facilitate radical changes in behavior, attitudes, and feelings. But it is not a panacea, and there are other important pieces of the puzzle, especially from a public policy standpoint. In order to get people to eliminate violence and other criminal behavior completely and permanently, a total transformation is required— not only for the individuals themselves, but in society. For example, the fundamental criteria we have established about what constitutes improvement in criminal behavior must be reevaluated.

I have serious reservations about most of the criteria that are commonly used to gauge improvements in criminals. For example, following his sixth session, one subject told me he had smoked coke with a woman on a weekend furlough. Because he had broken the rules of its program, the institution judged him to be doing poorly. But when the subject reported the incident to me, he stated that even while he was smoking the coke, he was asking himself, "What do I believe that is having me do this? If I can identify and eliminate the belief, I won't be tempted in the future. If I can eliminate enough beliefs, maybe I'll be able to resist my feelings." This thinking showed he had a greater sense of responsibility and commitment to true change than someone who goes through the motions of doing the "right thing" while incarcerated and is judged to be a model prisoner, but who knows that he probably will revert to his old behavior as soon as he is released.[3]

Even though TLM can assist incarcerated offenders to assume responsibility for their lives, improve the level of their self-esteem, eliminate criminal patterns of behavior, and create new possibilities for their lives, most of them also would need skills in order to survive after they were released from prison. For example, many might need assistance in writing résumés, looking for jobs, finding out about educational opportunities, and dealing with the family in which many of the beliefs were created (especially if they are teenagers still living at home).[4]

Offering this type of assistance to someone who still has the beliefs that lead to criminal behavior probably would make little difference. But once the beliefs have been eliminated, people become responsible for their lives and become open to, and usually very interested in, further assistance, which enables such assistance to be truly effective. It should be provided.

We must be clear, however, that using TLM for the rehabilitation of people who are already exhibiting criminal behavior is not enough. Prevention is the true goal. As Deborah Prothrow-Stith, M.D., Assistant Dean for Government and Community Programs, Harvard, recently pointed out, using the analogy of lung cancer:

> One would not propose a campaign to reduce lung cancer that focused only on treatment (tertiary); it is clear that better treatment will not reduce lung cancer rates. Helping people

who smoke to stop (secondary) and preventing people from beginning to smoke (primary) are essential. Most public policy discussions of violence are about tertiary strategies; whether to try juveniles as adults; whether to impose stiffer sentences, mandatory sentences, or three strikes and you're out.

Public debate and policy must move beyond the tertiary level and must include primary and secondary programs designed to prevent violence, and not merely to respond to it.

TLM was used in this study as a tertiary strategy. Used this way, I think it can significantly reduce recidivism, which I intend to demonstrate in a proposed research study. TLM can also be used as a secondary strategy by helping teens or even adults—whose beliefs predispose them to join gangs, sell and use drugs, and engage in violence—to eliminate those beliefs. Finally, it can be used as a primary strategy, by assisting parents to eliminate those beliefs that interfere with effective parenting.

After I finished my sessions at Maple Street House during the tenth week of the study, one of the residents said he wanted to talk to me. After he reminded me that he originally had volunteered for the study but had not been chosen to have weekly sessions with me, he asked for help.

"I keep breaking the rules here, and I'm afraid I'm going to get sent back to jail. People have been telling me my whole life that I do what I want to do when I want to do it, and I can't seem to stop myself. Isn't there any way I can get into your study so you can help me?"

It was one of the most frustrating and upsetting moments of my life. I had to hold back the tears. I knew that TLM could help him. In fact, it might be the only thing that would enable him to break the cycle that could send him back to jail. But there was no way I could have LBP sessions with him because he was in the control group. When I got home I told Shelly what had happened and resolved that somehow, no matter what it took, I would find a way to make TLM available to everyone who wanted it.

To the extent that this pilot study—along with all the other material in this book describing TLM —convinces the administrators of some drug and alcohol clinics, prisons, or alternative incarceration centers that TLM can be helpful, I would like to start training staff members at those institutions so they can offer the LBP to their residents.

Postscript

That Christmas I received a card from one of the fifteen-year-old subjects with whom I had worked.

Mr. Lefkoe I hope you and your family have a wonderful X-mas. Again I'd like to thank-you for all the help you gave me if it wasn't for you I just don't know what condition I'd be in right now. I prayed, prayed, and prayed that God would help me and he did he sent you thank you

Love,
Drew

Chapter 8

Case History Frank: Transcending AIDS

The highest use of the psyche in the course of human illness is not the cure, but for transcendence of the conditional events we call health and disease.
—Dr. Larry Dossey

"*Have you heard* about the new field of medicine called psychoneuroimmunology (PNI)?" my colleague Steven Hart asked me one day in 1988. "Based on recent PNI research, I'll bet TLM could be used to assist people with AIDS to improve their immune system." I was intrigued but skeptical. How could TLM possibly help the immune system?

Steven told me he knew some men in New York City who had HIV, the AIDS virus. Many of them also had full-blown AIDS. They were looking for alternative treatments and were interested in research on the effect of the mind on the body, specifically on the immune system.

Steven told me a little about the field of PNI. Some researchers were beginning to demonstrate a significant medical connection between the mind and the body's immune system. One pioneer in mind-body research, Robert Ader, a professor at the University of Rochester's Medical School, was quoted as saying, "There is little question that we can alter the course of disease by manipulating psychological factors."[1] And summarizing the research done in this area, *Newsweek* concluded:

With the help of sophisticated new laboratory tools, investigators are demonstrating that emotional states can translate into altered responses in the immune system....The logical next assumption would be that emotions have an impact on health.[2]

My AIDS Workshops

After my conversation with Steven, I got excited about the idea of using TLM with people who were HIV-positive or had full-blown AIDS to see if eliminating negative beliefs would improve their immune systems. I asked Steven if he would put me in touch with people who might want to do a workshop.

While Steven worked on enrolling people in the workshop, I started to do some reading. One of the first books I picked up was Bernie Siegel's then-current best-seller, *Love, Medicine & Miracles*. Dr. Siegel, a surgeon, had worked with groups of cancer patients to help them use their minds to deal with the illness. He had concluded, "The fundamental problem most patients face is an inability to love themselves, having been unloved by others during some crucial part of their lives." He went on to say, "Psychological shaping in the formative years plays a large part in determining who will develop a serious illness. Its effects are even more specific, however. It often determines what disease will occur, and when and where it will appear."[3]

This was intriguing because TLM appeared to be able to change people's "psychological shaping." I had already discovered that many people's childhoods led them to negative beliefs about themselves. Now I was finding out that those same negative beliefs could have a significant impact on physical health.

Dr. Siegel made the connection quite clear: "Other doctors' scientific research and my own day-to-day clinical experience have convinced me that the state of the mind changes the state of the body by working through the central nervous system, the endocrine system, and the immune system. Peace of mind sends the body a 'live' message, while depression, fear, and unresolved conflict give it a 'die' message."[4]

After reading that I couldn't wait to see if TLM would help people with AIDS.[5] We enrolled ten men who were HIV-positive, some with symptoms of AIDS. I faced them one Saturday morning, eager to see what would happen. "The purpose of our time together," I told them, "is to empower you with a technology—a tool you can use whenever you'd like—that will enable you to change your beliefs. This technology can be used to improve the quality of your life. I guarantee I can deliver that. Even though you might not be able to use TLM individually on yourselves, I'll teach you how to work with each other."

I paused and looked into their faces. "What I can't promise is remission of your illness. However, based on the available evidence, as you change your beliefs about yourself from negative to positive, your immune system should improve. If it gets back to normal, any illness that is a function of a breakdown in the immune system should go into remission. Will it? That's what we are about to find out. Given the scientific evidence, there is a lot of reason to think it could happen."

I then discussed the issue of blame or guilt. "Even if it is true that your illness is a function of your beliefs given your childhood environment, you couldn't have concluded anything other than what you concluded at the time. Now, however, you have a chance to change the beliefs. If that helps, great. If not, then there are still some things we don't understand about the relationship between beliefs and illness, but you have everything to gain and nothing to lose.

As we began to explore the beliefs in the room, the men came up with the typical negative self-esteem beliefs I've mentioned earlier, such as **I'm not good enough, I'm not worthy, I'm not deserving**. All of the men were gay and in addition to the usual self-esteem beliefs I had seen before, there were some other beliefs that seemed to stem from their experiences with being gay.

- **I don't deserve to be here, to breathe, to live.**
- **I'm unnatural, a violation of nature.**
- **The world is not a safe place.**
- **I have to hide the "real" [homosexual] me. It's not acceptable.**
- **I'm a despicable person.**

- **It's not safe to be alive. To be alive is to risk death** [at the hands of homophobic people].
- **The world is a dangerous place, and I can't defend myself.**
- **What I want doesn't matter, and it's not smart to draw attention to myself.**

The beliefs these men listed were the almost inevitable decisions people would make about themselves and life when their sexuality not only was judged morally wrong by much of society, but was also used as a justification for personal and governmental persecution and even physical abuse.

Shelly and I led several workshops and a number of evening follow-up sessions. We also had a number of private LBP sessions with a few participants who became committed to using TLM regularly. Several of them buddied up and had repeated sessions with each other. Those who did TLM with us or with each other reported significant emotional and attitudinal changes, but we had no objective measurements for changes in their mental or physical condition.

Less than a year after the first AIDS workshop, however, one of the participants with whom Shelly and I had a number of private sessions and who had also done sessions regularly with a buddy, told us that his Kaposi's sarcoma, a skin cancer that is a common manifestation of AIDS, had disappeared. He had stopped all medication. It was only one anecdote, which didn't prove anything, but it was still promising. (His skin cancer was still in remission when we last talked, five years later. He had no other symptoms of AIDS during that period.)

At that point, I decided to do some controlled research as a way of getting doctors and public health officials to pay attention to TLM as an intervention that could possibly help. I started contacting key people in the field of PNI, asking if they would be willing to participate in a research project that would determine whether or not TLM could produce enough change in beliefs, attitudes, and feelings to improve immune function.

There was very little interest. "What evidence do you have that your intervention will really eliminate beliefs?" I was asked. When I said I had only anecdotal evidence but wanted to pursue "hard" evidence through the study, the researchers lost whatever small interest they might have had. The dean of one New York City medical school asked me sharply, "What degree do you have, Mr. Lefkoe? An M.D., or a Ph.D. in psychology?" When I answered, "Neither" she hung up on me.

It took me a year, during which time I demonstrated TLM and talked to well over one hundred immunologists, physicians, and psychologists, before I was finally successful. Elinor Levy, Ph.D., an immunologist at Boston University, agreed to be a co-principal investigator. She helped me find Dennis Kinney, Ph.D., a psychologist at Mclean Hospital, Department of Psychology, Harvard Medical School, who became the other co-principal investigator. Dr. Kinney designed the study and prepared a fifteen-page research proposal. From that point, we went in pursuit of funding, a lengthy and often frustrating process. To this day, the study remains unfunded, but we still hope to raise the money eventually.[6]

Funded or not, I realized I could not give up on these men who were facing the most important fight of their lives. I felt a deep responsibility to continue my work with AIDS.

Transcending Illness

As I described earlier, the essence of TLM is not merely eliminating beliefs but creating yourself and living as the creator of your life. You live as a paradox, both as the creation and the creator, having the experiences of your life (as the creation) and, at the same time, knowing (as the creator) that you created them all. In this state of consciousness you have feelings, but you realize you aren't your feelings and you don't experience being controlled by them. You are able to witness your life, as opposed to being run by it. You respond to the events of the moment both positively and negatively, depending on how you assess them, but on some level you know that the assessments are not "real." They are only distinctions you have made up.

I had the privilege of having a client with AIDS who appeared to live almost continuously in this state. I would like to share with you how he got to it and what both he and I learned about health and illness during the two years we were friends and worked together.

Frank's Story

In the spring of 1989, Frank, who had been diagnosed HIV-positive, attended one of my Lefkoe Method workshops with his partner, Alan, who did not have the HIV virus. Early in November, Alan called to tell me that Frank had just come down with AIDS and was in the hospital. Alan explained that Frank had eliminated one belief in the workshop. Subsequently, Alan had done TLM with Frank and helped him eliminate a second belief. Now, Alan told me, Frank might be interested in working with me further, and Alan asked me to call him. When I reached Frank we talked for a while about TLM and my workshop. I told him I was trying to raise money for my research project and would let him know if I could use him in the study.

We talked again in early April, when it had become clear that the research would not be starting any time soon. I agreed to drive into New York City to work with him weekly without payment. It would be an opportunity to learn how TLM might be used most effectively with people who had already contracted an illness, especially AIDS. My sessions with Frank would make me better prepared for the study when I finally funded it. Also, Frank was very interested in spirituality and, more specifically in the relationship between TLM and spirituality. Based on his two earlier experiences with TLM, he had the sense it could be valuable for him.

During our first session I suggested that we do what I normally do with clients: work on some dysfunctional pattern in his life that he would like to change, rather than working directly on his illness. He had already eliminated the belief **I'm not good**

enough and the accompanying survival strategy belief **What makes me good enough is pleasing others**.

Now, Frank described a pattern that bothered him: "I use sarcastic, flippant, glib humor to mask my insecurity. I use it to take the offensive. I use it to negate compliments. If I get loving, supportive comments, I do this to deal with the fear that it will be taken away."

The beliefs he identified and eliminated during our first session that were driving the undesirable pattern were: **People are going to leave me** and **I have to rely totally on myself**, which are a basic belief and a survival strategy he devised to cope with the reality created by the initial belief.

During the course of our sessions, Frank described additional undesirable patterns: "I withdraw from situations where I feel joy and support; I sometimes feel I can't trust the people in my life" and "I've never felt good enough creatively in whatever I was involved in, even skating [Frank had been a famous professional ice skater], so I worked harder than anyone— compulsively. I distrust myself. I love doing creative work, but I doubt that it's good enough."

How Being Gay Affected Frank's Life

Early on, we discussed how Frank thought being gay had affected him. We spent a lot of time talking about that and about his early experiences.

"As a kid I was more feminine than other boys, and other kids called me a sissy. They said I wasn't like them. I've felt persecuted since I was a kid. I never even tried to fit in, and I felt hurt when I was left out. I was always sensitive, which other boys my age saw as a weakness. I loved and listened to classical music as a young child, under ten. I didn't like rough physical sports. I felt as if I didn't fit in in grade school. I felt comfortable with the feminine side of me by age six or seven—maybe younger. I was very much alone in grade school. By high school I developed a strategy to be accepted and liked.

"Expression of my sexuality was never a big deal. I had no problem drifting from men to women. When I was famous and being interviewed, I couldn't express my sexuality publicly. I'm more open now, but I still hold back. One reason I moved to New York City was because being gay here was more accepted. How safe would Alan and I be in our suburban home or in most southern cities?

"Society as a whole doesn't accept my sexuality. I feel persecuted from time to time. It's not safe to be gay at my gym. Given the conditions in society and my sexuality, I have to modify my behavior. I can't express myself freely in public because it's not safe. Society would never accept me if it knew who I really was.

"I've never been accepted by the community of life. The world is unaccepting, hard, and has no sense of priorities that appeal to me. The world's priorities are so totally out of whack that there's no way they could support human life: greed, competitiveness, money, position in the world, rigidity, inflexibility, lack of compassion.

"There's a type of straight man who repulses me and always has. He's macho, inflexible, rigid. I equate him with the world. People like that are not open to differences in the world, differences in people. My image of that type of man is of a conservative, southern military man. He is afraid of sensitivity, compassion, heart, intuition. He has a lack of acceptance of different lifestyles."

I asked Frank specifically how he felt about being gay. His answer was similar to that given by almost every gay man I've talked to: "I'm okay being gay, but it's not okay in this world."

Some of the beliefs that arose from Frank's experiences:

- **It isn't safe for me to express who I really am.**
- **I can't be loving, expressive, and open in this world.**
- **If I expressed myself totally my life would be threatened, because gay people are considered deviant, perverted.**
- **The world, society, life are unyielding, unaccepting, tyrannical, prejudicial, hostile.**

- **The real world is inhibiting and suppressive of me and my vision.**
- **I can't be me in the world.**

The Lesson of AIDS

Over a period of several months, using TLM, Frank eliminated these and other beliefs about himself and life. At some point we started talking about his illness.

"AIDS is lethal. It's killed off several friends and lovers," Frank said. "But in a funny way it's been a gift, too. It's forced me to totally reconsider my life. There's a reason why so many people have AIDS, and a reason why the type of people who have it have it. It's like I've agreed to be part of some sort of cosmic lesson. I was a prime candidate. I had changed careers, given up figure skating, which had been the most important thing in my life; my best friend broke up our relationship; my lover died of AIDS."

"If AIDS is a lesson for you personally, what is it?" I asked Frank. He had a list:

- It forced me to look at life in a more spiritual way.
- It gave me a sense of urgency to discover what's real and important in my life, to be really honest about my life.
- I have freedom to create my own time. My boss is allowing me to work my own hours.
- I didn't feel up to dealing with what life was dumping on me. Now I don't have to push as hard in the ways I used to.
- I have more patience, understanding, care from my boss, my friends, and my mom. No deadlines now. No pressure.
- I don't have to put myself through the "struggle." If I didn't have AIDS there might be the tendency to have to prove myself.

"Two years ago," Frank told me, "there was no way to express myself and no relationship. I felt, 'What's the point of living?' I seriously thought about suicide several times. Now at my job (he worked part-time publishing a company newsletter), I touch people in a way that they're better for it. I'm here to be a catalyst, to affect, help change people's emotions, effect change on an emotional level. I have the ability to touch people's hearts. When I connect with people, somehow my life is different. People experience joy. I have a sense of acceptance. I can allow people to be light about their lives. Accept themselves in a more loving way. Provide opportunities for others to grow in a more loving and accepting manner. Touch people emotionally. I'm closer to my vision now than I've been in quite a while. I'm picking up where I left off when I was thirteen years old."

Seven months after our first session I spoke to Frank's employer to see what changes he saw in Frank. "There has been a change over the past few months, an improvement in his mental attitude toward life," his boss said. "He smiles more. Frank has a positive attitude toward people on the staff. He used to have less of a personal relationship with others. Now he relates more warmly."

After nine months Frank told me, "I feel an ongoing sense of comfort around my spirituality. Something has changed through our work. It's comforting. Death will be a good experience. It doesn't worry me. Our work is reaffirming my spiritual beliefs. I carry that with me on a daily basis. At this moment the idea of living longer or shorter doesn't seem important; I'm not worried about dying right now. I'm doing things emotionally and spiritually that I should be doing."

After we had been working together for about ten months, Frank remarked, "I don't experience myself as a 'sick person.' I have a sense of peace about myself. Since the last session I've been experiencing life as a duality, a drama that I can choose to get involved in or not."

A month later he said, "If I died tomorrow I would have learned the lesson I needed to learn in this lifetime."

After eleven months, I talked to Alan about how Frank was doing. He told me, "Frank's emotional and self-concept levels have never been stronger. Rest, peace, forgiveness of others. Both from my observation and from what he's said, it's clear he's never had anything like the perspective that this work offers. And his physical deterioration is still proceeding. He has an infection on his neck, swollen legs, his lesions are getting darker. The oncologist has lightened treatment again. Frank expects that another emergency might be the end."

When I next saw Frank, I told him what Alan had said and asked if he agreed. He nodded and added "I'm not living out of 'I'm going to die.' I'm in great emotional, psychological, and spiritual shape."

Frank Transcends His Illness

Ken Wilbur, who has written extensively about transformation, made an observation that captures the essence of Frank's attitude:

> Thus the individual's mind-and-body may be in pain, or humiliation, or fear, but as long as he consents to simply abide as the witness of these affairs, as if from on high, they no longer threaten him, and thus he need no longer manipulate them, wrestle with them, subdue them, or try to "understand" them. Because he is willing to witness them, to look at them impartially, he is able to transcend them.[7]

After a year, during which he had about forty sessions and eliminated many beliefs, Frank was getting weaker so we weren't meeting as often. Despite the fact that I thought Frank was in better shape psychologically and spiritually than most of the people walking the streets of New York City, his body still wasn't getting better. And that's what I had hoped to be doing with Frank: helping him get rid of or at least halt the progression of AIDS. I searched for books that might provide me with clues. I spent hours looking for possibilities I hadn't yet seen. What beliefs had we not gotten to? What aspect of his life had we not looked into deeply enough? What attitudes did long-term AIDS survivors have that Frank didn't have? What beliefs could be eliminated that might open up the possibility of gaining those attitudes? What could I do that I hadn't yet done? I was frustrated and upset. I had grown to love and admire Frank very much, and I was unable to help him get better as I had originally hoped.

In a conversation just one year after our work started, Frank told me, "I'm able to experience and express feelings and anger. Self-expression is okay. If I could stand up for long enough periods of time I'd be painting. I don't think people will leave me. I'm secure in feeling loved. I no longer have the sense of being a victim of my father's behavior. I've come to terms with feelings of abandonment by my mom. I'm very secure with Alan; he's here for the long haul. I trust he will not abandon me. I make my needs and opinions clear to him. I never would have described myself as a victim a year ago, but in retrospect I know I was." The person Frank was describing was almost the opposite of his description of himself a year earlier.

Although we talked on the phone from time to time, I only had two additional sessions with Frank. Then in October he called and told me he was back in the hospital. He had lost the sight of one eye and his body had deteriorated badly. Amazingly, he was still in good spirits. We made an appointment to have a session in the hospital a few days later. When I arrived at about 10:00 A.M., a nurse stopped me outside the door and asked, "Are you a member of the family?" I was afraid she wouldn't let me in if I said I wasn't, so I just nodded and walked on without waiting for permission. Alan was sitting on the bed, his eyes red from crying.

"Frank passed away less than an hour ago," he told me tearfully. We looked at each other for a moment and then hugged. We talked about Frank for a long time—how much we both loved him, how he'd changed in the past year, and how he'd actually enjoyed the last months of his life.

I had started working with Frank a year and a half earlier with the sole purpose of helping him eliminate beliefs so that his immune system would improve enough to halt the spread of AIDS in his body. That was what I thought TLM had to offer. Given my original purpose, Frank's death should have meant total failure. But I didn't feel failure. There was a greater truth in evidence.

Later, when I read a piece by Larry Dossey, it was as if he had Frank in mind when he wrote it:

Future forms of therapy that emphasize the potency of the mind in the origin and course of human illness will recognize [the importance of transcendence] . . . . They will utilize psychological interventions to more effectively and humanely treat illness, but with the added understanding that there is yet something more important for the patient to learn. They will rightly acknowledge a state of health that transcends the problem at hand or any illness that might develop in the future. They will proclaim that the highest use of the psyche in the course of human illness is not for cure, but for transcendence of the conditional events we call health and disease, birth and death.[8]

Life Is about the Journey, Not the Destination

My work with Frank helped me to discover something important about TLM and about life—something I had only known intellectually before our time together: Life is about the journey, not the destination. TLM had not kept Frank alive, but it had supported him in his spiritual quest. He had been able to change most of the behavior patterns that had diminished the quality of his life. He had been able to eliminate his negative sense of self, so that he could accept and enjoy himself without concern for what others thought of him. He had been able to forgive his parents and others he thought had harmed him in the past. And, most importantly, he had created himself as the creator of his life and had been able to live in that space much of the time during the last year of his life.

I regularly quote to people one of Frank's statements when I am trying to explain the experience of living as the creator of your life, as opposed to living as the creation. I tell people that, when asked how he was feeling, Frank always answered, "My body's in terrible shape. But I am in great shape."[9]

Part Three

Re-creating Our World

Chapter 9

Raising Empowered Children

It's not really difficult to get your children to do what you want them to do, if the punishments are severe enough. But at what cost to the rest of their lives?
—Shelly Lefkoe

"Why can't you ever?" "How come you never?" "Surely you realize!" "Did you?" "Can you?" "Will you?" "Won't you?" "Aren't you?" "How many times do I have to tell you?"[1]

Imagine that you're a young child hearing these words from your parents over and over again, day after day. How do you think you would feel?

If you are a typical child, you'd feel guilty, sad, angry, resentful, and ashamed. But more than that, you would begin to form beliefs about yourself based on your conclusions about what those statements meant. And what would you be likely to conclude? **There's something wrong with me. I'm not good enough. I'm not worthwhile.**

Most parents would be horrified to realize that their daily words might result in the formation of such beliefs. They mean well. They do the best they can. How could their children respond with such low self-esteem beliefs?

Perhaps TLM has something to offer. The primary purpose of this chapter is to assist parents—those people who have taken on the most important and most demanding job in the world—to become more effective at that job. A secondary purpose is to help anyone who wants to understand the relationship between the disastrous state of the world and how the people in the world have been (and are still being) parented.

This chapter is dedicated to the children of the world, with the intention that it contribute to their future well-being.

The "Job" of Parenting

My wife, Shelly, used to complain that when men at parties asked her what she did, and she answered, "I raise my two children," the men would turn away, bored—as if a mom wouldn't have anything very interesting to say. Now Shelly tells people she is a professional mother. The response is usually surprise: "What is a professional mother?" She replies that her primary job is "mother," and she trains and studies for that job the same way other professionals prepare for theirs.

It's fascinating that people would respond to Shelly's description of her "work" with such surprise. For virtually every job you've ever held, you've received some formal or informal training or education—either initiated by you or by the organization for which you worked. But if you decide to become a parent and take on one of the most difficult jobs imaginable, there is no training required. You're expected to know what to do automatically. This is absurd! It is no more obvious how to parent than it is how to treat an illness, draw up a contract, or be an effective administrative assistant.

About five years ago, Shelly created a business, the Possibilities of Parenting Center (POPC), designed for parents, teachers, mother's helpers, and others who work with children. Her company offers workshops and private LBP sessions that help people become better caretakers for children. POPC's mission is: "To have parents discover that self-esteem (the experience of being able and worthy) and a positive attitude toward life are the key to children's happiness and success, and to empower them to assist children in the creation of self-esteem and other positive attitudes."

Although Shelly and I have read a great many books and have taken a number of workshops on how to parent more effectively, our best parenting lessons have come from facilitating people using TLM. Session after session, hour after hour, we have heard people describe the experiences they had with their own parents that led them to dysfunctional beliefs: "My Mom and Dad always did. . . they never did . . . they always said. . . they never said."[2]

What our parents do and don't do, say and don't say, provides us with the experiences that we interpret into beliefs. Those beliefs, in turn, create our reality and determine our lives— for better or for worse.

In our workshops, we help parents discover:

1. What they want for their children

2. That getting what they want for their children depends on their children having healthy self-esteem and a positive sense of life

3. That their children's self-esteem beliefs result primarily from interactions with their parents

4. That the essential function of parents, initially, is to assist their children to create positive conclusions about themselves and life and then, when children reach their teen years, to help them discover that they are the creators of their lives

Let's first walk through the essence of our workshop. Then we will examine some beliefs you might have about parenting and the relationship between them and the above four points.

What Do You Want for Your Children?

Take a piece of paper. Title it List A at the top and write down your answer to the question: What do I want for my children? In other words, how do you want their lives to look as adults? If you could choose the three most important characteristics or qualities that you would like your children to have when they are ready to go out on their own, what would they be?

Some answers that other parents have given include: self-disciplined, responsible, self-reliant, good study habits, self-motivated, good feelings about him/herself, good values, self-confident, sensitive, secure, high self-esteem, kind and caring, considerate of others, good relationships, happy with spouse and children, and financial success.

Once you write down what you want for your children, the next question is, "What can you do to help them turn out that way?" Write down on another piece of paper, titled List B, your answer to the question: How do I behave with my children on a daily basis, so that ultimately they will turn out the way I want them to? I'm not asking you what you think you should do but what you really do. What behavior would someone see if they looked through your window and you didn't know they were there? What is some of your typical behavior—that you're happy about and not so happy about? Write your answers on List B.

Some answers that other parents have given include: nag, yell, explain, make happy, threaten, play with, show, punish, make time-outs, praise, teach (good manners, neatness, good study habits), coddle, reward, and plead.

Now look at List A and ask yourself which of the two following types of beliefs would be more likely to produce the qualities you listed: (1) **I'm not good enough; I'm not okay; there's something wrong with me; I'm not worthwhile; people can't be trusted; life isn't fair.** or (2) **I'm good enough; I'm okay just the way I am; I'm worthwhile just because I am, not for any reason; people can be trusted; life is open to my having whatever I want.**

It probably seems obvious that what you want for your children would be impossible to fulfill with the first set of beliefs. In fact, as we discussed earlier, these are beliefs that lead to such dysfunctional behavior as drug and alcohol abuse, teenage pregnancy, the inability to have a close and lasting relationship, gang membership, anxiety and depression, and the inability to experience real inner satisfaction.

That being the case, the next question to answer, on a third paper headed List C, is: What behavior would enhance my children's healthy self-esteem and a positive sense of life?

Some answers that other parents have given include: checking rather than directing, exploring possibilities, encouraging, acknowledging, giving respect, modeling, allowing risk-taking, being on their side, giving choices, listening, showing unconditional love, providing a sense of security, trusting, and being honest.

Now on a fourth sheet, titled List D, write your answer to the question: What behavior would inhibit my children's healthy self-esteem and positive sense of life? (If you have trouble answering this question for yourself, you might think about what other parents do or what you've observed.)

Before you answer the question, let me emphasize that inhibiting behavior isn't necessarily "unloving." For example, Shelly's parents are two of the most loving people I've ever met. They love her—and loved her as a child—as much as a child can be loved. Her parents were committed to her life being wonderful all the time. Whenever she tried to do something new as a child, such as pouring milk, setting the table, or helping with the dishes, they said, "That's okay, honey. Let me do it." They didn't teach her to bake, cook, sew, or do other similar things that her friends were learning. After hundreds of experiences like this, what do you think Shelly concluded about herself, despite the love that motivated her parents' behavior? She decided: **I'm not capable.**

The issue here isn't your intentions, but your behavior.

Some answers that other parents have given include: accusing, directing, blaming, judging, spanking, characterizing, labeling, demanding, comparing, being too busy to spend enough time, criticizing, overprotecting, martyrdom-sacrificing, inconsistent love, conditional love, not acknowledging, unreasonable expectations, rescuing, and denying feelings.

Now place the four lists in front of you. List A is what you want for your children. List B is how you behave with your children. List C is behavior that enhances a healthy self-esteem and positive sense of life. List D is behavior that produces a negative self-esteem and sense of life.

Your children's success, as you defined it, requires healthy self-esteem and a positive sense of life. To what extent is your behavior, List B, closer to the inhibitors on List D than the enhancers on List C? Can you see that at least some of your behavior is not likely to create the positive self-esteem beliefs that are required for your children to have what you say you want for them? Can you see that your behavior sometimes inhibits the creation of a positive self-esteem?

List A	List B	List C	List D
What do I want for my children?	How do I behave with my children on a daily basis?	What behavior would enhance my children's healthy self-esteem and positive sense of life?	What behavior would inhibit my children's healthy self-esteem and positive sense of life?

You Aren't a Bad Parent

The purpose of this exercise is not to have you discover that you are a bad parent. If you are like most parents, you love your children and you are committed to their well-being. You want to do the best you possibly can. However, if you are a typical parent, you've had little or no training in that role. Naturally, sometimes your behavior enhances and sometimes it inhibits positive self-esteem. The point is not to criticize the number of inhibitors you exhibit, but to help you to reduce them and increase the number of enhancers.

You may want to change your behavior, but because it is the result of your beliefs, the first step is to discover the beliefs that are driving you. Then you need to eliminate the beliefs so that the new, desired behavior will come naturally.

What do you believe, probably unconsciously, that could explain the inhibiting behavior on List B? Each of you will have to answer that question for yourself, but some typical answers are: **My job is to produce results. . . . . My job is to teach my child how to achieve success. . . . My job is to make my child happy.** Can you see how one or more of these beliefs might result in your inhibiting behavior on List B? Don't you use those behaviors to get your children to listen, to do as they're told, to learn what you think they should know, and even to have what you think will make them happy?

Most parents believe: **I've succeeded as a parent if my behavior with my child produces the desired result, teaches the desired information, or makes my child happy.** But ask yourself: At what cost? If you succeed in achieving what you want, and, as a result of your interaction, your child forms negative self-esteem beliefs, was your behavior really "successful"? Is what you achieved short-term with your child worth the long-term cost?

I'm not saying that your children's behavior on a daily basis, their learning, and their current happiness are not important. Of course they are. What I am saying is that the single factor that has the greatest impact on whether or not your child achieves what you wrote on List A is a healthy self-esteem, a positive sense of life, and other positive beliefs such as **Relationships work. . . . It's safe to express feelings. . . . People can be trusted.** Nothing they do, learn, or feel as a child will have as much influence on their lives as the fundamental beliefs they form and take into adulthood.

The Major Role of Parents

Given the crucial role of beliefs, what do you think the major role of parents should be? Influencing behavior, teaching information, and making their children happy? Or helping their children to create positive decisions about themselves and life?

If you chose the latter—which I believe is much more important—the best way I know to ensure that you are doing your job well is to constantly ask the question: What is my child likely to conclude about herself and life as a result of the interaction we just had? If it's a positive belief, congratulations! You got your job done. If it's a negative belief, go back, apologize, and clean it up.

What clients report during LBP sessions provides parents with bad news and good news. The bad news is that you have to be very careful about what you do and say with your children, because your behavior is the model from which your children will create the beliefs that determine the rest of their lives.

The good news is that nothing you do as a parent actually *determines* how your children's lives will turn out. Only a person's interpretations/beliefs determine their reality—not the earlier experiences on which they are based. And beliefs can always be changed. It's inappropriate to blame your parents for the way your life turned out, because individuals *always* have the power to change beliefs that are determining their lives. Remember, every person is both the creation and the creator of the creation.

Beliefs that Cause Inhibiting Behavior

Let's take a look at some of the most common beliefs parents have that lead to inhibiting behavior. If you're a typical parent, many of them will sound familiar to you.

Belief One: I Am Responsible for My Child's Behavior

When my daughter Blake was ten, I saw her take a friend's hat and I immediately told her to give it back. A few minutes later, I began to wonder about my action. Why did I tell Blake what to do? If her friend got angry and didn't want to be friends with Blake anymore, that would be a good lesson for her about respecting other people's property. And if her friend didn't get angry, then it was just a game and Blake would give the hat back on her own. There were half a dozen other possible outcomes. Why did I feel I had to make sure she gave the hat back right away?

I discovered after a little exploration that I believed **I am responsible for my children's behavior toward others.** And if I am responsible, then I have to constantly monitor her dealings with others.

Once I had identified my belief, the next question was: What conclusion would Blake eventually come to if I continued this type of behavior long enough? Possibly, **There's something wrong with me** (because Dad is always telling me what to do and not to do). Or, **I need someone else to make sure I do the right thing**. (With this belief, what would happen when someone told her that "everyone" was trying drugs or having sex? If she couldn't count on her own judgment, she would have to listen to what everyone else was saying.) The belief that you are responsible for your child's behavior toward others inhibits the development of independence and a healthy self-esteem in your child. Your intention may be benevolent, but the result is to foster self-doubt.[3]

Your beliefs as a parent determine your behavior, which lead to your children's beliefs, which in turn, determine their behavior. The best place to break this cycle is with your own beliefs as a parent. If your children have already reached adolescence and have formed their core self-esteem beliefs, you need to help them eliminate those that lead to dysfunctional behavior.

Belief Two: Children Should Have the Same Standards of Behavior as Adults

On another occasion, Brittany, then age four, took about ten pieces of Scotch tape from my desk and put them on her bedroom walls and furniture. I asked her to not take any more tape because she was wasting it. She repeated her behavior on several more occasions, and I found myself getting increasingly annoyed because she wasn't listening to me. "Brittany," I warned her, "if you keep taking my tape, you won't be allowed in my office anymore." Unfortunately, the threats didn't faze her.

At that age, Brittany seemed to march to her own drummer. It was hard to enforce any rules. At meals, she would always half-sit, half-stand, as if she were getting ready to take flight from the table. I must have said "Sit down!" ten times a meal. I was always nagging, cajoling, and creating "consequences."

Finally, I asked myself, "What is Brittany concluding about herself and life as a result of these interactions?"

One possibility might be: **I can't do what I want to do in the world; I need someone else's permission**. And perhaps also: Daddy's constantly unhappy with what I do, so **There must be something wrong with me.** Or: **Others know and I don't**.

I began to think about what I believed that produced my anxious, nagging behavior. When I finally discovered it, I realized that it was a belief that a great many parents had: **Children should have the same standards of behavior as adults**.

Putting several inches of tape on the wall is wasting tape by adult standards; it is a game by a child's standards—and a very inexpensive game at that. Standing during a meal is not polite by adult standards, but children are filled with energy and have a hard time sitting still at any time. In fact, there is a lot of evidence that children can pay better attention if they are permitted to move around than if they are forced to sit still for long periods of time. (Many schools have successfully dispensed with the standard fixed desks and allow children to sit, lie, walk around, stand, and kneel during classes with excellent results.)

A child who is repeatedly told; "Don't do this, don't do that!"—when merely doing what is natural for a child that age—experiences the criticism as personal invalidation rather than parental instructions not to do a specific thing. That child will probably conclude, **There is something wrong with me; I can't do anything right, so why bother?**

And a child who is feeling angry (or upset, or any other feeling) who is repeatedly told, "Don't be sad. . . . You're not really angry at your friend; she didn't mean it.. . . That shouldn't upset you" or "Don't cry" will most likely hear the injunctions as, **There's something wrong with the way I am. . . . What I feel doesn't matter.. . . or I can't trust my feelings**.

The consequences of the beliefs formed as a result of interacting with your children this way are children who experience their limitations rather than their unlimited potential; children who feel bad about themselves; children who have a sense that life is too much for them and that getting what they want will be difficult, if not impossible; children who believe that what they feel, want, and do isn't really important.[4]

Belief Three: Children Can't Be Trusted

When my daughter Blake was five she constantly complained that she didn't want to eat what Shelly and I were having for dinner. One day, I suggested to Shelly that we try an experiment and allow Blake to eat whatever she wanted, given that we only kept relatively healthy food in the house. Shelly thought I had lost my mind, but I insisted that Blake could be trusted. Shelly argued that she was not old enough to be trusted. After a long and heated discussion, Shelly agreed to an experiment. For two weeks Blake would be allowed to eat whatever she wanted that we had in the house.

The next morning Blake got up and asked for ice cream for breakfast. Shelly was so upset that she served the ice cream and then left the kitchen so she wouldn't have to watch Blake eat it. The next day Blake went back to her typical health food cereal for breakfast. Although she decided to eat what Shelly and I had as a main course for dinner most evenings, she asked for and received a sweet dessert every night, usually ice cream. After a few days she started saying to us, "I'm not going to have ice cream tomorrow." But the next day she invariably had ice cream.

One evening about ten days into the experiment, the three of us were in our car driving when Blake said to us, "Mommy and Daddy. I have a problem."

"What is it, honey?" I asked.

She sounded sad. "I'm eating too much sugar, and I can't stop myself."

Shelly looked quickly at me and then said to Blake, "How can we support you?"

Blake answered, "I still need you to say 'no' to me. We need to call the experiment off until I'm older."

Shelly had tears in her eyes. She told me later that she realized that she had been right in that Blake wasn't old enough to decide on her own what she could eat. But Shelly also realized that ultimately I was right because Blake could be trusted—if not to be able to control what she ate, then to ask for assistance in controlling herself.

What did Blake conclude about herself over this and similar incidents? I'm not sure, but probably something like: **I can be trusted. I am capable of deciding what works for me.**

What would a child conclude if she constantly heard her parents say, "I can't trust you to. . ." or observed behavior in her parents that implied a lack of trust? Probably: **I can't be trusted. I can't decide on my own what's best for me. I'll probably mess up unless someone tells me what to do.**

Belief Four: I'm the Boss

. One particularly detrimental parenting belief is: **We do it my way around here because I'm the parent**. In other words, "I'm the boss, just because I'm the mother or father."

There are a hundred times a day when a child asks, "Can I have a snack?" "Can I have a friend over?" "Can I watch TV?" or Do I *have* to?" There is no objectively "right" answer to many of these questions. Often the answer is arbitrary. Sometimes you give one answer, sometimes another. Why one or the other? No reason; it's just what you feel at the moment. Or, even if you think you have a reason, just as good a case frequently can be made for the opposite response. If your child challenges you and asks, "Why?" you may respond, "Because I'm your father (or mother)."

When the answer is arbitrary, why do we think that we need to retain the authority to provide the answer? Why don't we say instead, "What do you think? Why do you think that?"

Again, what conclusion would children probably reach if what they want is overridden frequently by the arbitrary commandments of their parents? How would they probably interpret continually asking, "Why can't I?" and hearing their parents answer, in effect, "I don't need a reason; I'm your mother (or father)"? Such a child may think, **What I want isn't important. I have no control over my life. I don't matter. Reasons aren't important, only power is important.**

Belief Five: My Job Is to Produce Results with My Children

This belief, perhaps more than any other, robs people of much of the joy of parenting, and it leads to negative beliefs on the part of their children. Many parents believe that the most important thing in any given interaction with a child is achieving a specific result: finishing the book that is being read, brushing the teeth, playing a new game by the rules, getting dressed, or eating a meal. One underlying parenting belief that could produce such behavior is **My job is to produce results with my children**. This belief is probably accompanied by the related belief **A successful parent is one who gets children to obey**. (Don't most parents of young children consider the ultimate accolade to be "Your child is so well-behaved!"?)

As a parent you probably find yourself frustrated and upset when your children want to do something other than what you want them to do. If getting your children to exhibit specific behavior and to complete tasks is your goal, you are doomed to frustration and upset because children often won't cooperate. Your annoyance comes from the assumption that the point of brushing teeth is to get the teeth clean; the point of playing a game is to complete it while observing the rules; the point of reading a book is to finish the story. Why? Who said so? You did. But children do not usually have the same standards as their parents. If you were to change your belief, most of the upset would disappear.

Remember the last time you heard a parent say, "My kids are wonderful, they always obey me." Or, "They never talk back." Or, "They are never a problem." Did you sigh with envy and say, "Oh, I wish my kids were like that"? Think again. What beliefs would a child have to have to always obey, never talk back, or never be a problem? Jane always did what her parents wanted when she was a kid. Her parents described her as "the perfect child." Two beliefs underlying her behavior, which continued to affect her later in life, were **What I want doesn't matter. I'm not important.** Norman was praised constantly by his parents for being so well-mannered as a child. He had concluded; **The way to be accepted is to make people happy and to never upset them.**

How do you think beliefs like these would affect your children when they become adults?

What if you decided that the primary purpose of every interaction was to assist your children to create positive beliefs about themselves and life?

When Brittany was young, it was a running battle to get her teeth brushed at night. Sometimes she'd resist going into the bathroom. Other times she'd refuse to open her mouth. Or she'd bite the toothbrush, or turn her head, or jump up and down. I was constantly annoyed that I couldn't get her to do what I wanted her to do, and I let her know it. At some point, I recognized the principle we're discussing here and I changed my focus to having fun during this activity, rather than completing it. When Brittany didn't want to go to the bathroom to brush her teeth, I'd ask her how she would like to go to the bathroom—with me leading a parade and her following, with her in my arms or on my back—or did she want to meet me there in five minutes?

This change occurred in other areas as well. Before, if Brittany interrupted me to talk about various things while I was reading to her, I'd try to get her to stop talking so I could finish the book. Again, I would feel annoyed because I was being frustrated in achieving what I had as my goal. I thought, isn't reading to children important? After changing my belief, I discovered that when I used the time we were in bed with a book to allow Brittany to talk about whatever she wanted, we had some very interesting and fun conversations. Our time together became more meaningful to both of us. And, most importantly, Brittany was probably forming positive rather than negative beliefs about herself and life.

Belief Six: I Have the Power...

Perhaps the most common parenting belief, the one that underlies all others, is **Parents have the power to determine how their children's lives turn out**. Consciously you might acknowledge that it is out of your hands, but take a look. Doesn't your behavior imply that you think your actions and statements can determine your children's behavior? Don't you think you are having a valuable and lasting impact on your children when you teach them table manners, good study habits, how to clean their rooms, and how to relate to others?

Most of what children do and feel when they grow up is not a function of what they learn or feel as a child. It is a function of the beliefs they form, both as children and later in life. Although you can provide a model of life that can influence those beliefs, you cannot control the beliefs. In fact, trying to control their behavior, or even their beliefs, more often than not produces an environment in which negative self-esteem and sense-of-life beliefs are created.

Jackie's mother and father were very successful professionals. From everything Jackie told me, it was clear that her mom and dad were loving, well-meaning parents. They wanted only the best for her. They often expressed their love and rarely yelled at her. They were determined that she be as successful as they were, which they thought would make her happy. No matter what Jackie accomplished, her parents pointed out how she could have done better. Jackie was corrected constantly; her parents were always showing her "the right way"—that is, their way, to do everything. She frequently heard as a child, "There's no need to make the same mistakes we made." What do you think Jackie concluded from her parents' behavior? **I'm incapable of doing things on my own. There's something wrong with me**.

Human beings, especially children, generalize about their experience. Instead of merely noting what we observe, we almost always ascribe meaning to our observations. Because there is no meaning out there in the world, our conclusions are always arbitrary and are never "the truth." Parents, therefore, have an almost impossible job: We are responsible for creating an environment in which children are more likely to form positive self-esteem and sense-of-life beliefs, but, no matter what environment we create, we cannot control the decisions children make.

The Beliefs That Lead to Child Abuse

Not only are many of our beliefs about parenting the source of ineffective parenting behavior, our own negative self-esteem beliefs and accompanying survival strategy beliefs are the source of the worst type of parenting behavior, child abuse. Two case histories involving parents who were verbally and physically abusive make this point very real.

Harold complained of his inability "to control my temper when my kids don't behave the way I want them to behave. I finally stopped spanking them, but I still lose control and yell at them when they don't meet my expectations."

In looking for the beliefs that produced this behavior, Harold realized that he felt powerless and out of control when his children didn't listen to him. He discovered the survival strategy: **Being in control makes me okay**, and the underlying belief **I'm not worthy**.

The highlights of his childhood experiences that led to this negative self-esteem belief included: "Mom said she felt her job was to point out what the kids do wrong. I'd always hear from her: 'How many times do I have to tell you? Aren't you ever going to get it right?' There was very little physical or verbal affection or warmth. I spent very little time with my mom."

In the other case history, Peter described his pattern as "yelling at my kids, when they fight among themselves, when they aren't obeying, when they don't listen to me."

He said that just before he yells he feels that he needs "to be in control to feel good about myself. When the kids don't obey, I feel out of control."

His underlying belief was **I'm powerless**. His survival strategy belief was **Being in control makes me powerful**.

Other LBP sessions with parents who report similar patterns reveal that child abuse frequently (if not always) is the parent's way to feel in control at a time when he or she feels out of control. The experience of being out of control can result from the children not listening or from other events in life. When a parent has negative self-esteem beliefs such as **I'm powerless** and a survival

strategy belief like **Being in control makes me** ρ
out of control brings the self-esteem belief to the su
with the anxiety that is associated with it. Verbally aι
abusive behavior with children (and even spouses) is th   ι to
get back in control, in order to cover up the anxiety paren ιeel
when they experience being out of control.[5]

Victims Create Victims

A great many adults act as if they believe that someone or
something outside themselves has ultimate power over them. They
think, "My life would be perfect if only my spouse (or my children,
or my co-workers, or my boss) would..." In other words, these
people feel they are victims of others. Where does that come from?

In addition to the constant "do this" and "don't do that" that
we hear as children, we also frequently hear, "You make me angry
[or some other feeling]!" The message is that something outside of
us determines what we feel.

Between constantly hearing "no" and "don't" and the
message that feelings are a function of something outside of you, it
is understandable that people would wonder, "Who am I to
determine how my life turns out?" Concluding **I don't matter** or
I'm powerless is virtually inevitable, given how so many of us
were brought up.

Pause for a moment. Is the connection between our
parenting styles and the state of society getting clearer? Can you
see that virtually all the problems individuals experience—from
drug and alcohol abuse, to crime, to relationships that don't work,
to people blaming everyone and everything else for their lives not
working and experiencing no personal responsibility for changing
their circumstances—are the inevitable result of beliefs that were
formed in childhood—and those beliefs were the inevitable result
of how we were parented and are parenting our children today?
You might not like this explanation, but if you are willing to accept
responsibility as parents, you have the opportunity to change your
parenting. You also have the opportunity to be a part of changing
the state of the world.

We can find confirmation in the stories of some of the great creators in history. Leonardo da Vinci's father was bothered by the way his son's interests seemed to change from month to month—first drawing, then engineering, then science, then nature. He concluded that his son couldn't stick to one area and would never amount to anything. Da Vinci's father didn't realize that his son was preparing to be a Renaissance man, who would be a genius in all of those fields and more.

As a boy, Albert Einstein was a daydreamer. He started speaking relatively late and did poorly in mathematics. Picasso was always drawing on walls—a behavior considered unacceptable, to say the least. Thomas Edison was constantly taking things apart that he couldn't put back together again; as he got older, he began conducting chemistry experiments that exploded in the cellar.

There's no question that the parents of these men spent many anxious hours and days worrying about their sons' "dysfunctional" behavior.

Today, these stories give us pause. If we try to change our children's behavior, we might well be trying to change the very behavior that is necessary for our children's unique "appropriate" development. If, however, we focus on assisting our children to create healthy self-esteem and a positive sense of life, we will avoid curtailing the so-called "problem" behavior if it really is appropriate.

Obviously, if your children are doing or feeling something that is disturbing to *them*, you can help to eliminate the belief that is producing what they consider undesirable. Also, if their behavior clearly harms them, someone else, or something of value, you need to discuss that behavior with them.

You Still Need Skills

Even after you have examined your beliefs regarding parenting and have eliminated those that are likely to result in inappropriate interactions with your children, knowing how to interact with them in a way that facilitates a healthy self-esteem and a positive sense of life is not self-evident.

What should you do after working on your beliefs? Study. Study. And then study some more. Support groups with other parents can be very useful. There are a great many excellent books, along with a number of workshops available throughout the country that provide excellent strategies and skills. (See Suggested Reading for a list prepared by Shelly's POPC that should be helpful.)

A reminder: Skills are useful to people only when the skill is consistent with their beliefs. Skills are not useful to people whose beliefs make using the skill unlikely or impossible. In other words, as long as you have beliefs like **As the parent I'm the boss** or **My job is to produce results with my child**, you won't be able to use the skills to facilitate positive beliefs consistently. Learning how to listen is irrelevant if you think your job is to tell, not listen. If, on the other hand, you have eliminated such beliefs and have concluded that your job as a parent is to assist your children to create positive beliefs, you will be able to make good use of the skills you learn from books, workshops, and support groups.

Moreover, you might discover as I did, after reading a few books designed to provide the skills for being more effective parents, that the lessons are just as valuable in dealing with adults. In fact, after reading *Liberated Parents, Liberated Children* by Adele Faber and Elaine Mazlish, I remarked to Shelly that if one substituted the word "manager" for "parent" and "employee" for "children," it would be an excellent textbook for managers.

I've asked myself from time to time, "Do we need to learn special skills for raising children, or would it suffice to change our beliefs about ourselves, life, and relationships so that we treated all people appropriately?"

And wouldn't it be a worthwhile principle to ask ourselves, after interacting with anyone, "What might the other person conclude about himself or herself and life as a result of my interaction?" If we behaved with everyone so that the conclusion was always positive, or, if negative, that we apologized and cleaned it up, would there be much more we had to learn about dealing with children and teenagers?

Although such an approach certainly would be a significant improvement over the current state of much parenting, I think some skills still would be needed. It's not obvious how to deal with children so they reach positive conclusions about themselves and life as a result of your interactions. Some knowledge of child development—for example, what is age appropriate—certainly would also be necessary.

I've learned this the hard way with my daughter Blake, who is now a teenager. Blake and I have always been very close. She has felt safe discussing with me whatever was on her mind, and I assumed that I would be able to raise any subject or issue with her. That was the case until she turned eleven. Then, all of a sudden, communication shut down.

It started when I suggested she watch a television program for adolescents about sex. She reacted ferociously. Not only wouldn't she watch it, she wouldn't even discuss the idea of watching it. That was the beginning. Then, it all came to a head one week when she was almost twelve.

She'd had a few dates with a twelve-year-old boy in her school. She wouldn't talk to me about the boy, the dates, her feelings, or anything remotely related to the issue. When Shelly or I tried to talk about it, she got annoyed and refused to discuss it. When she came home from school, she took the phone from my bedroom to hers and closed the door. She didn't come out for hours. I had a hard time getting her to talk to me about school, her friends, or almost anything else in her life. She got angry with Shelly and me for not allowing her to go with her friends to a local mall without an adult present, and she was withdrawn and non-communicative about everything for almost a week.

Nothing like this had ever happened before. Blake was no longer the daughter I had known for almost twelve years. She had shut me out almost totally. Our close relationship had been one of the most important things in my life, and it looked to me as if it had disappeared. I was hurt. No, I was devastated! I walked around in a daze for almost a week.

I tried hard not to see it as wrong of Blake not to communicate. But I wasn't very successful. And, although I tried to keep her from feeling guilty by telling her she wasn't doing anything wrong and that I would figure out what I believed was making me so upset, she probably felt responsible to some extent.

In an attempt to understand adolescence better, I got some books that described this stage of development. I had concluded that something had gone wrong in my relationship with Blake, which was terribly upsetting to me. As I started reading, however, I realized that nothing was wrong, either with Blake or with our relationship. What I had seen as withdrawal from me was natural behavior in this new stage in Blake's life. I discovered that the essence of adolescence is asserting independence from parents. As soon as I realized there was another interpretation for Blake's behavior, my upset disappeared. As I became more understanding of Blake's behavior, I was better able to support her by letting her go through whatever she needed to go through. It became okay with me that she wasn't communicating with me. In a few weeks things were back to normal, and communication had reopened between us.

Obviously what I did during that week didn't permanently damage Blake or our relationship, but had I known what to expect before it happened, I probably would have been able to handle my reaction to her behavior a lot sooner.[6]

When you are a parent, you are (or should be) in a constant state of learning, growing, and developing. By eliminating your inhibiting beliefs and learning effective parenting skills, you can make the experience of raising children so much richer. And what could be more rewarding, ultimately, than helping your child to develop healthy self-esteem and a positive sense of life?

Chapter 10

Organizations That Thrive on Change

Rapid knowledge-based change imposes one clear imperative: every organization has to build the management of change into its very structure.
—Peter Drucker

Immediately after I created TLM, I started using it to empower groups of employees to shift the way they saw their jobs. Except for the initial Carter Hawley Hale assignment, which I referred to in the Prologue,[1] I had never actually used TLM one-on-one in a corporate workshop. I was concerned that businesspeople would be unwilling to discuss dysfunctional patterns, beliefs about their self-worth, and their childhoods in front of their peers.

Then Larry Moon, the CEO and owner of Kondex, a small manufacturing company in Lomira, Wisconsin, heard a presentation I made and called me several days later. He told me he would like to retain me to work with his seventy employees, but first he wanted to make sure that his management team was fully on board and supportive of the idea.

"Can you come out for a day and give my top people a preview of what you'd do in a two or three-day workshop?" Larry asked. He said he hoped my presentation would convince his managers that workshops for all their employees would be valuable.

I said sure. I was confident that I could make a convincing presentation. The next week I flew to Wisconsin.

Sitting informally around the table with the small group of Kondex executives, I began to explain how TLM worked to change employees' beliefs about their jobs. Suddenly, Larry spoke up.

"Can you show us?" he asked. "I'll be the guinea pig and do TLM right here."

I tried to warn him that we couldn't know before he stated his pattern what the belief might be that gave rise to it, and we wouldn't have any idea where the belief came from until we started looking. He didn't seem to care. "That's okay, let's do it."

Much to my amazement, he named a pattern that uncovered a self-esteem belief leading back to his childhood and his parents— right in front of the three members of his management team! Before I knew it, the others had done it too. It *was* possible to have businesspeople do TLM in front of their peers. I knew my work with organizations was about to take a quantum leap forward.

During the workshops with the seventy Kondex employees, a few of them felt uncomfortable doing TLM in front of their colleagues, and a few of them even had a hard time watching others. But, virtually everyone who participated found the experience extremely powerful and beneficial. They not only could see how it could be used in business situations, they saw new possibilities in their personal lives as well. Once you see yourself as the creator of your life, you see new possibilities everywhere you look.[2]

The Key Is the Culture

As I worked with corporations I began to formulate a theory about corporate change that would become the foundation for my work. This theory, and the consulting approach that flowed from it, has become a remarkably successful tool for corporate change. It will ultimately take an entire book to explore all the principles and success stories. However, I will give you an overview of what I have learned and experienced.

Early on I realized that the behavior of individuals on the job is not just a function of their own distinctive personal beliefs, it also is determined by the beliefs they share with their coworkers— namely, the organization's culture.

By "culture" I mean an organization's fundamental beliefs about how to deal successfully with its environment and the circumstances it faces. A culture becomes visible in the innumerable policies, practices, procedures, organizational structure, management style, and systems. I call them P's and S's. The behavior of employees in an organization is ultimately determined by its culture. In fact, an organization will find it virtually impossible to implement any strategy—marketing, financial, or otherwise—that is inconsistent with its culture.

Let's examine the culture of companies in just one industry, department stores, to clarify this point. Most department stores believed for decades that the way to survive and succeed was to offer the right products, priced correctly and presented well. In other words, the culture was based on a focus on product, price, and presentation.

How does such a culture show up in their P's and S's?

- Salespeople are hired primarily to take customers' money; their effect on a sale is considered minimal.

- Salespeople are compelled to spend much of their time on labeling and stocking rather than with customers.

- Salespeople are poorly compensated and have virtually no prestige in the company, which leads to considerable turnover.

- The important people in the organization are the buyers, who choose the "right" products.

- Management learns all it needs to know about customers from computer printouts of what was purchased.

- It seems irrelevant to find out directly from customers what truly would satisfy them.

- A minimal amount of time is spent discussing customer satisfaction in management meetings.

For decades, department stores operated successfully with a culture based on "product, price, and presentation" and its corresponding P's and S's. Then one day in the 1980s many woke up and discovered that they were in serious trouble. Some were forced to declare bankruptcy. A few decided they ought to try a new way of operating. They noticed that a chain of department stores called Nordstrom was expanding rapidly at the same time that they were deteriorating.

Why was Nordstrom successful? It had a very different culture from the typical department store. It did not believe that the best way to survive and succeed was products, pricing, and presentation. Although these were important, Nordstrom believed the way to succeed was to provide extraordinary customer service. Its salespeople, called associates, had the authority to accept returns without sales slips, to deliver items directly to customers when needed—in short, to do whatever it took to satisfy customers. The most important people in Nordstrom's stores were the sales associates—those who came face-to-face with the customers.

What would be the chance of instituting an approach like Nordstrom's in a conventional department store? Given the culture in place, slim to none. The type of salespeople hired, their training, their other duties, and the lack of focus on customers would make it virtually impossible for a Nordstrom-style approach to succeed. If a department store wanted to implement the Nordstrom strategy, it would first have to change its culture.

This principle explains why GM, IBM, Sears, and many other major corporations lost their industry leadership and incurred significant losses: Their cultures and their P's and S's prevented them from successfully implementing the new strategies that were required by a rapidly changing world.

Creating Real Change

In order for a corporate culture always to be responsive to its environment, there needs to be what I call Third Order Change.

I'll define that concept by first discussing what constitutes First and Second Order Change.

First Order Change is characterized by a change in behavior that is consistent with the existing belief or culture. First Order Change usually consists of finding ways to do things a little better, faster, or easier. It produces incremental improvements that are consistent with the existing culture and its P's and S's. One example would be a service technician using a new tool to install, fix, or maintain equipment. Using the new tool might make his job performance better or his task easier, but it would still be entirely consistent with the way the service technician already sees his job as a technical employee. That's First Order Change.

In chapter 1 we saw how Information + Motivation was a formula incapable of producing fundamental change. That formula, however, is capable of producing First Order Change, because the desired new behavior is consistent with the same belief. All you're doing is trying to effect change within the existing box.

Second Order Change is characterized by behavior change that requires a new belief or culture. The desired behavior is inconsistent with the existing belief and requires a new one to open a different set of behavior possibilities that didn't exist before. An example would be service technicians who see themselves in a box labeled "technical people." They're really unable to take care of customers because that role is inconsistent with the way they see their jobs. In Second Order Change, they would create a new job belief—**I am a customer satisfier**—in which taking better care of customers becomes possible. The shift in belief would allow employees to see taking care of customers as part of their job instead of getting in the way of their job.

Second Order Change is fundamental rather than incremental change. Whereas First Order Change consists of improving what already is, Second Order Change consists of creating something totally new. It is starting with a blank sheet of paper. In Second Order Change the existing belief must be eliminated so that you can take a fresh look at the current environment and form another belief that is appropriate for today.

An excellent example of Second Order Change can be found in *Re-engineering the Corporation* by Michael Hammer and James Champy. It concerns Wal-Mart and a single product, Pampers, the disposable diaper, a bulky item that needs a lot of shelf storage space relative to its actual dollar value.

Wal-Mart maintained Pampers inventory at its distribution centers, from which it filled orders. When the distribution center inventory was low, Wal-Mart would reorder more diapers from Procter & Gamble.

But the business of managing inventory was complex, and Wal-Mart struggled with devising a formula that would put enough Pampers on the shelves to satisfy customers without creating a storage problem. The Wal-Mart management approached Procter & Gamble with a proposal that P&G, which probably knew more about diaper movement through warehouses than Wal-Mart, should take on the task of informing Wal-Mart when it needed stock.

P&G agreed, and the plan was implemented. Each day, Wal-Mart would tell P&G how much stock it was moving out of the distribution center to the stores. When P&G felt it was appropriate, it would tell Wal-Mart that it was time to reorder and how much. If the recommendation seemed to make sense, Wal-Mart would approve it and P&G would ship the goods.

Hammer and Champy wrote about the result: "The new arrangement worked so well that over time Wal-Mart suggested that P&G henceforth skip the purchase recommendation and just ship the diapers it thought Wal-Mart would need. In other words, Wal-Mart offloaded its inventory replenishment function onto its supplier."[3]

In the process, Wal-Mart cut inventory costs and increased the effective management of stock. The idea was an unmitigated success. Managing their inventory better, cheaper, or faster would have been First Order Change on Wal-Mart's part. Second Order Change consisted of starting from scratch as if there were no inventory system at all and asking: Given today's technology, supplier capabilities, cost structure, and competition, what is the best way to handle our Pampers inventory?

It is important to emphasize that in Second Order Change you can't know exactly what the new behavior will look like when you create a new belief, be it personal or organizational. The new box creates possibilities that didn't exist before. Although you might have a sense of what some of those possibilities are, there is no way to know what all of them are until they are explored. When you operate out of a new box, you figure out what to do in each situation, limited only by your imagination and the restraints of the new box.

For example, when service technicians create a new job belief—**I am a customer satisfier**—they become committed to satisfying customers. At the moment the belief is created, however, neither they nor their manager knows for sure exactly what the new behavior will look like. In fact, each "customer satisfier" will devise his or her own new ways of satisfying each customer.

Here are a couple of examples to clarify the difference between First and Second Order Change.

Assume that an autocratic boss who always controls everything in the department suddenly starts delegating major responsibilities to subordinates. At first, it may seem to be behavior consistent with fundamental Second Order Change. But think about it: Who decides what will be delegated and to whom? Who decides if the work is being done right? Who has the authority to take the work back? Even though the change might have seemed fundamental at first glance, in reality the basic relationship between manager and subordinates has not changed. This is First Order Change—different behavior but the same box.

Here is another example. A few years ago when Quality Circles were set up in some companies, everyone was very excited about them and called them a fundamental change. Quality Circles gave employees a chance to meet together in groups, on company time, to discuss changes they wanted to have made. They were told that their contribution to corporate policy was highly valued. But what happened to the recommendations the Quality Circles made? They were handed over to some manager, who decided which suggestions to implement and which to discard. That's the way it had always been. True, employees did get together in groups and it was on company time, but that was merely First Order Change—a different way of arriving at suggestions inside the old box.

This is not to say that First Order Change is not valuable. Very often all that is required is for employees to do their job a little differently—and First Order Change allows that to happen. But we should be clear that merely doing things differently inside the old box is not fundamental change.

How do you know if a company requires Second Order Change? I always ask employees in my corporate workshops, "What percentage of your time do you spend creating value for customers, and what percentage of your time do you spend getting through the culture—the P's and S's—so that you are able to create value?"

They answer that from 50-95 percent of their time is wasted dealing with the culture. When employees look to see what is wasting their time, they discover how the existing culture and its P's and S's act as a barrier to the work itself. It is often a startling realization: The company itself is preventing them from doing an effective job!

Companies run into a problem when they try to produce Second Order Change with a technique that is only able to produce First Order Change—namely, Information + Motivation. As I explained in detail earlier, Information + Motivation rarely produce out-of-the-box change. Why? Because we think we saw with our eyes what we believe. Logical arguments, threats, and promises will not overcome what we think is the evidence of our senses and eliminate existing beliefs. Producing Second Order Change requires a different approach, which TLM provides.

Third Order Change

In a world that didn't change very frequently, an organization that was able to create Second Order Change probably would do very well. But in a world where what works in business today is probably out of date by next year, even Second Order Change is insufficient.

Although Second Order Change opens new possibilities far beyond those that had existed before, you still end up assuming that the new beliefs are as true as you used to think the old beliefs were. At that point you are as locked into the new beliefs as you were with the old ones.

Third Order Change is similar to Second Order in that the required new behavior is not possible in the existing box. Unlike Second Order Change, however, where a company gets out of old boxes in order to get into new and better boxes, the Third Order Change company is never in a 'box" at all.

Third Order Change results from always operating out of *questions*—such as, What's needed to succeed today?—rather than *answers* regarding the right way a company or worker should act in order to succeed. An organization characterized by Third Order Change is one where most of the employees recognize that there is no ultimate truth about business.

They operate as if everything will need to be changed as the environment changes. You could say that a culture characterized by Third Order Change is a meta-culture. In other words, it is a culture that develops whatever specific culture is appropriate for each unique environment.

Just as your ultimate personal goal is not merely to eliminate beliefs but to create yourself as the decision maker, so the ultimate goal for an organization is to recognize that it, too, should make up its culture and all of its P's and S's appropriate to the environment at any given time. Operating in a new and better box produces Second Order Change. Operating as the box creator results in Third Order Change.[4]

The Necessity of Third Order Change

We currently are living in a world that is changing rapidly and fundamentally. As William B. Joiner, a partner in the consulting firm of Action Management Associates, has pointed out:

Change itself has changed. Change and turbulence have become constant features of the external environment. As a result, contemporary organizations . . . need to develop, first and foremost, the capacity to adapt continually to ever-changing conditions in ways consistent with their ultimate purposes. . . . The great challenge for leaders is to develop learning organizations.[5]

In his recent book, *Managing in a Time of Great Change*, Peter Drucker, the renowned management thinker and consultant, points out that:

The new jobs require, in the great majority, qualifications the blue-collar worker does not possess and is poorly equipped to acquire. . . . They require a different approach to work and a different mind-set. Above all they require a habit of continuous learning. . . . At the very least, [workers] have to make a major change in their basic attitudes, values, and beliefs.[6]

Ask yourself, "What are the possibilities of adapting and learning if you believe you already know 'the truth' about the world and how to deal with it successfully?" The only way to learn is to recognize that there is no "ultimate" answer and that you can't ever stop asking questions. That is TLM thinking, which would result in Third Order Change.

Continuous improvement is, by definition, a process, not merely a state change. Second Order Change merely substitutes one state for a better one. An organization committed to continuous improvement requires Third Order Change, which is a state of constant flux and change.

Many people have commented that my description of a Third Order organization sounds similar to what most companies do when they are just getting started. They don't have many P's and S's. People change what they do easily. It is true that most new organizations don't espouse very many "the truths." But, Third Order Change organizations know there is no "the truth," whereas new organizations think there is and are looking for it. When "the truth" is discovered by such organizations, they will be institutionalized in P's and S's.

People and Organizations Don't Resist Change

If you really analyze the nature of—and differences between—these three types of behavior change, you will come to a startling conclusion: human beings and organizations really don't resist change!

"Nonsense," you might reply. "Look at all the evidence of resistance." I will admit that people and organizations do resist something, but is it change?

Here's an exercise to provide an insight into my claim. Try to follow the instructions as closely as you can, and you'll discover something fascinating about change and resistance. Imagine that you really believed there is no "the truth" about business, that there is no right way to do your job, that what you are doing today is only the best solution you could find for today's circumstances. Imagine you also believed that under significantly different circumstances you and your colleagues should and would operate differently.

Now imagine that a year or so from now you discover that the circumstances that affect your job—such as the competition, technology, and customers' needs—have changed dramatically. Would you have a hard time changing the way you do your job?

To the extent that you really believe there is no right way to do your job, you would not resist changing your behavior when you noticed a change in your environment.

So what is it that people do resist? If you think what you are doing now is the right thing to do, and then someone tells you to do something different, how does it appear to you? Well, if you believe that your current behavior is *right*, you believe that the advice you're getting is *wrong*. You're not really resisting change so much as *resisting doing what you think is wrong*.

A Third Order organization would welcome change because change would be its greatest competitive advantage. Other organizations initially wouldn't see changes in the environment as they occurred. Eventually they would acknowledge the environmental changes and try to deal with them. They'd start with First Order Change. Eventually, some of them might make Second Order Changes. By then, what would have happened to the environment? It would have changed even more. They would never be dealing with the world as it is at the moment.

As Eric Hoffer, the San Francisco longshoreman philosopher, once put it: "In a time of drastic change, it is the *learners* who inherit the future. The *learned* find themselves equipped to live only in a world that no longer remains." (Emphasis added.)

Who are the people best able to identify what needs to be done at any given time regarding a specific job or function? More often than not, it's the people who do the job. Thus, a Third Order organization is one in which most employees operate as if they are responsible for creating the culture that is most appropriate for implementing their mission, given any particular environment.

Employees in a Third Order organization would be monitoring the environment constantly to see which changes, if any, they would need to make in the future. As they observed the world changing, employees would change the company's P's and S's and their personal beliefs about their jobs—except their "beliefs" would be not be held as "the truth" but rather "a truth."

What is required today for all organizations—in business as well as in nonprofit firms and government—is a culture that welcomes change, instability, and operating from questions rather than answers. What's needed today more than ever before are cultures that continue to adapt to a constantly changing external environment.

I like the word used by Frederick Kovak, vice president for planning at Goodyear: "The key term is 'reconfigurable.' We want an organization that's reconfigurable on an annual, monthly, weekly, daily, even hourly basic. Immutable systems are dinosaurs."

Why Cultures Get Stuck

In earlier chapters we saw in detail how personal beliefs are formed and eliminated. It's much the same with organizations. The same basic principles of TLM are used to eliminate cultural and other business beliefs, but I use a variation of it in organizational settings.

Here's a football story I often tell in workshops that shows how organizational cultures get formed, and the variation I use to assist employees to change them.

Consider a professional football coach who has just been hired. What is his job you might ask? Win the Super Bowl as quickly as possible. How would he start? He'd look at all the relevant aspects of his environment: the players, the coaches, the competition in his division, the competition outside of his division, and so on. After his analysis of the elements of the environment, he'd make whatever changes he could to improve them. Finally, he'd need something that would determine his playbook and virtually everything else he did for the rest of the year. What is that? Not an all-pro quarterback, although that certainly would help. What he needs is a game plan—a belief that one strategy has a better chance of getting his team to the Super Bowl than any other.

Assume that he chooses a ball-control ground game. (You don't have to understand football or what a ball-control ground game is to follow this story.) Now assume further that he wins the Super Bowl. What should he probably do next year? Most people, including a lot of coaches, would say: a ball-control ground game. Why? The answer you'd get from most fans, players, and coaches would be: because it works.

You are now about to discover how it's possible for a team to win the Super Bowl one year and not even make the playoffs the following year. If the coach's strategy is really the reason the team won the championship, then it should work the next year. But what if several of the best assistant coaches, who made the ball-control ground game work, leave to go with other teams? What if a few of the players crucial to the ball-control ground game become free agents and leave, and a few others are injured? What if you're able to obtain a quarterback known for his ability to throw long, and an all-pro wide receiver? What if the competition knows what you did last year and is designing a game plan specifically to stop you from doing it again? In other words, what if there is a total change in the environment that originally led the coach to conclude that a ball-control ground game was the best strategy?

What makes a coach successful over time is not the specific strategy he chooses in any given year but the questions he asks of his environment that lead him to his strategies. If he does that the year after winning the Super Bowl, he will be able to choose the most appropriate strategy for that year. It may be the same strategy and it may be totally different. In either case it will be chosen in light of the anticipated environment; it will not be repeated merely because it worked before.

This analogy applies to the way organizations form their cultures. They look at the competition, customers, employees, and technology to decide how best to survive and succeed. When they succeed, they look at the evidence of their profit-and-loss statement and conclude: **The best way to run a business is to . . .**

Once they believe this is the "right" way to run a business, they either don't look into the environment anymore to see if it has changed, or they do look, but through the filter of already knowing what they will see—which prevents them from noticing when there is a meaningful change.

Consider the story of Compaq computer. It was one of the fastest growing, most successful companies in history during its first couple of years; a few years later it was in serious trouble. For doing what? The very same thing that had made it so successful initially! The world in which it operated had changed, and Compaq had not.

Let me continue my football story to describe the way we frequently try to change beliefs and behavior in organizations. Imagine that you are in the stands immediately following the Super Bowl game, and your team has just won. You are very excited, but you are concerned about next year. Several of the best players and coaches will not be back. The competition now knows what to expect. The environment will be very different. So you decide to go to the dressing room and discuss your concerns with the coach. Somehow you manage to get in to see him.

"Congratulations!" you say to him.

"Thanks." He grins. "Have some champagne."

"Coach," you say, "I'm a little worried about next year. I think it might be a mistake to use the ball-control ground game again—" Before you have a chance to finish, the coach pulls the glass of champagne from your hand and you are shown to the door by a couple of burly security guards.

As silly as this sounds, isn't this how most behavior changes are presented to workers by their managers? "Don't do what you're now doing anymore. You should be doing something different." Or, if we're very sophisticated: "Don't believe what you believe anymore. You should believe something different about your job." Although workers are rarely in a position to show their managers to the door, they probably feel just as resistant and angry as the coach who won the Super Bowl.

In order for coaches or corporate employees to be able to look at the current environment and really see it, the existing belief must be eliminated.

How to Get Cultures Unstuck

Now consider how you could get the coach to consider a different game plan next year by using a variation of TLM. You walk up to the coach and say, "Congratulations on winning the Super Bowl! How did you do it?" (What is the current pattern of behavior?)

"Weren't you watching?" the coach replies. "We had several drives where we held the ball for over six or seven minutes each. They only had the ball for about twenty-two minutes."

You nod. "I did see that. It was great. But what was your strategy or game plan that enabled you to accomplish that?" (What belief produced that behavior?)

"We executed a brilliant ball control ground game," he answers.

"Of all the possible game plans you could have chosen, whatever gave you the idea to employ that particular strategy this year?" (What did you observe in the environment that led to that belief?)

He assumes his coaching demeanor. "At the start of the season I looked carefully at the players we had, their strengths and weaknesses, and I made a few good trades and acquisitions. I got rid of a few assistant coaches and got a couple new ones who were great. I then did an analysis of our competition. Based on everything I saw after I finished, I decided that a ball-control ground game was the way to go."

"Let me get this straight. You decided on a ball-control ground game because of the specific circumstances at the start of the season?"

"That's right. And I made a damn good choice, didn't I?"

"You sure did! By the way, coach, aren't you losing your head defensive coach and several other assistant coaches?" (Instead of looking for other possible interpretations of the circumstances that led to the belief, the variation in TLM used in organizations is to ask if the current environment is the same as the one in which the belief was formed.)

"Yes, but I'm sure we'll be able to find good replacements."

"Aren't we losing a lot of the players on offense who enabled us to ground out one first down after another and, on defense, who always got the ball right back? Some won't return next year, a couple are injured, and a few are getting pretty old."

"That's true. But I'm sure we'll be able to pick up players who'll be just as good."

"What about the competition? I noticed they had seven or eight men on the line most of the time, anticipating our ground game."

"It was getting more difficult as the season progressed, but we created a few surprises out there today and we'll find a way to do the same next year."

"Let me get this straight, coach. You said that you created the ball-control game plan because of the specific environment you observed at the start of the season. Now you say that significant elements of the environment are almost totally different. Based on the type of analysis you did last year, what game plan do you think you ought to employ next year?" (If the current belief is a function of the old environment, and the environment now is very different, what belief and behavior would be appropriate now?)

"That's a good question. I'll have to think about it during the off season."

Can you see the difference in the two approaches? In the first case, you told someone they shouldn't do what they were doing, which produced resistance and defensiveness. In the second case, you didn't tell anyone anything. You only asked questions designed to allow the other person to discover that what he thought was "the truth" for all time was only "a truth" at a specific time.

Also, can you see that in this scenario you aren't using TLM as I've presented it? You are using a different process based on the principles of TLM. Instead of looking for other interpretations or explanations for the events that are the source of the belief, which will lead to the belief disappearing, you clearly see that the belief was a perfectly logical and valid interpretation of a specific set of environmental factors. Then you look to see if the environment has changed. Realizing that your belief is the result of interpreting a unique set of environmental conditions and that those conditions have changed radically will have the belief disappear. If the environment has changed, you then do the same thing you originally did: interpret the environment that is currently in front of you.

A Third Order Shift in Fundamental Beliefs

In her excellent book *In the Age of the Smart Machine*, Harvard professor Shoshanna Zuboff writes:

> The 21st century company has to promote and nurture the capacity to improve and to innovate. That idea has radical implications. It means learning becomes the axial principle of organizations. It replaces control as the fundamental job of management.[7]

In other words, a fundamental shift needs to occur in business—from getting people to act differently (according to management dictates) to having them think, innovate, and create on their own. When all the employees have access to the information that used to be reserved to the privileged few, they can and do use it to make the organization more competitive and successful.

Here's an example. Gary Reiner, GE's vice president of Business Development, reports:

> GE's big breakthrough has been giving workers flexibility and unprecedented authority to decide how to do their work. All the good ideas—*all of them*—come from the hourly workers. At GE Power Systems, a $6.8 billion unit that makes generating equipment, changes in production methods cut inventory carrying charges by $90 to $100 million a year. (Emphasis added.)

More evidence: After an ALCOA magnesium plant in Addy, Washington, fed production data back to the factory floor, workers quickly found ways to boost production by 72 percent.

These extraordinary levels of improvement require not old-style workers, who merely do different things as dictated by management, but a transformation of the workers' functions—from carrying out instructions to identifying and initiating what needs to be done on their own.

Two fundamental beliefs that managers and workers have about their jobs need to be changed in order to create a Third Order organization.

1. Most managers believe that their job is to figure out what workers should do and then get them to do it.

2. Most workers believe that their job is to do what their managers want as best they can, without trying to change the P's and S's under which they operate.

In order to create a Third Order organization:

1. Managers need to believe that their job is to create an environment in which workers do the thinking that they, the managers, used to do. Then they need to support workers in making the changes they propose.

2. Workers need to believe that their most important job is to figure out what barriers (in other words, what P's and S's) are getting in the way of them doing their jobs. Then they need to eliminate them.

In workshops, I always ask participants what limitations there would be for them if they created a Third Order organization. Their answer, stated with amazement, is always the same: "There wouldn't be any limitations!"

Just as an individual in the space of the creator experiences no limitations and infinite possibilities, so, too, employees in a Third Order organization who operate as the creator of the company's culture and P's and S's experience no limitations and infinite possibilities.

Why Managers Tell People What to Do

One common belief that I frequently hear in workshops is: **The job of managers is to figure out what workers ought to do and then get them to do it. If managers don't tell people what to do, nothing will get done.**[8]

My experience is that most supervisors and mid-level managers who have had their jobs for at least fifteen years have this belief. Given the current trend in many organizations to have managers listen to and empower their workers instead of "boss" them, this belief often gets in the way. The ability to assist managers to rid themselves of this belief would have a significant impact in many organizations.

The following "case history" is a composite of a number of different sessions with managers at several companies.

Most managers who choose this belief to work with generally state it as a fact, as something that is so obviously true that the manager isn't sure what there is to talk about. What else would a manager do?

"Okay," I say, "you think this belief is the truth. Where did this idea come from? What did you experience in your life that led you to this belief?"

The answer is always some version of "I see it every day"— and then they tell their daily war stories.

"I'm sure you do see it every day," I respond, "but what was the earliest experience that led to the belief? What happened yesterday isn't the source of the belief, because you believed it the day before yesterday, didn't you?"

They usually refer to their first job, sometimes a part-time job in high school, sometimes a summer job, sometimes a first job after college. I ask them to describe what happened.

"Well, there was this guy, the manager, who told us what to do and how to do it—and then we did it. Sometimes, when he wasn't around, we goofed off. And when he was around, we worked harder." I probe a little. "Did many of the workers initiate work that the manager didn't ask for?"

"A couple of workers sometimes, but most of us just did what we were told to do."

"Did you know what to do before the manager told you?"

"No."

"Did most of the other workers know what to do before the manager told them?"

"No."

"So what did managers do at your first job?"

"They told people what to do."

"And what did workers do?"

"What the managers told them to do."

"So your belief—**The job of managers is to figure out what workers ought to do and then get them to do it. If managers don't tell people what to do, nothing will get done**— was a logical conclusion for you based on your first job experience, wasn't it? It wasn't a silly or irrational conclusion. It really made sense, didn't it?"

The managers respond, "It sure did."

"Let's play a game," I say. "It's called Possibilities. Let's see if we can find ten possible explanations for, or interpretations of, what you observed in your first job, other than what you concluded. We aren't looking for a better explanation. The one you came up with is as good as any we'll find. But let's find ten more."

It only takes a few minutes to find them.

1. All the managers at that company told people what to do, but that might not be true at all companies.

2. The workers at that company only did what they were told to do, but at other companies they might do more on their own.

3. Managers acted that way in that industry, but not necessarily in all industries.

4. Those specific ten or twenty workers and managers I worked with acted that way; other workers and managers might not.

5. That behavior occurred in the particular corporate culture that existed at the time. It might not occur in any other type of corporate culture.

6. That behavior occurred in the United States. Managers and workers in Japan, Germany, or some other country might not exhibit that behavior at all.

7. That behavior occurred in the 1950s (or 1960s, or whenever), but it might not occur at another time in history.

8. Teenagers exhibit that type of behavior, but older workers might not.

9. Workers on their first job usually do only what managers tell them to do, but as they progress in their careers they might take more responsibility for their work and initiate things on their own.

10. That behavior occurs when you have workers who haven't had much training. If workers get training in what to do and how to do it, they might not need much supervision.

By this point it is clear that what the managers saw on their first job could be interpreted in several different ways, each one just as valid as the next.

"Can you see that what you concluded was a valid interpretation, but that it was no more valid than any of the others?" I ask.

"Sure."

"Didn't it seem to you at the time that right there on the factory floor or in the office, right next to the manager who was telling you what to do, you saw this 'thing' called **The job of managers is to figure out what workers ought to do and then get them to do it. If managers don't tell people what to do, nothing will get done**?

"Yes, I saw it." They nod.

"Is it clear now that you never saw any such thing 'out there'?"

"Yes."

"Well, if it didn't exist 'out there,' where was it?"

"It was an interpretation in my mind."

"So," I ask, "is it 'the truth'?"

They laugh and say: "No. It isn't."

It usually takes less than half an hour for a manager to eliminate this belief about the need to tell people what to do in order to get any work done.

Then I ask, "Can you imagine your job being any different when you get back to work?"

"Yes. I see the possibility of asking workers instead of telling them. I see that they might have a lot to contribute that I never realized before. I see that I could be their partner instead of their boss. I see that perhaps I have better things to do than look over their shoulders. I see that I have to look at each individual worker to determine how much guidance he or she needs; there is no one truth about all workers under all circumstances."

A Corporate Application

Let's see how to apply the modified LBP as I presented it in the coaching story to the culture of the Information Services (IS) department of a large corporation. If you were to ask members of a typical IS department to describe their behavior, they might say, "We determine what hardware and software everyone in the organization needs, then we purchase and install it. We write custom programs. We also maintain all hardware and software. We determine priorities."

The next step is to find out what beliefs produce that behavior. In one organization I was told:

- We need control.

- Every piece of hardware must be connected to the mainframe.

- We need to purchase the software.

- The role of the end users is to tell us their problems so we can solve them.

- We must decide.

- We are the experts.

- We develop solutions in response to customer needs.

Can you see how an IS department's behavior can be totally explained by these beliefs? The next question is, "What is the source of these beliefs? What happened that led to those beliefs?" IS employees who have been around since the late 1970's and early 1980's will respond that when the department originally was created:

- There were very few people in the company who knew what they really needed from IS.

- We only had mainframes; PCs were used only for analysis, not general business purposes.

- There were no off-the-shelf software packages; we had to create all the code for our own software.

- There were few contract programmers; we had to do it all ourselves.

- Our clients' (that is, the other departments) needs didn't change frequently, so what we created worked for many years.

- Most clients knew very little, if anything, about how computers worked.

- Most people in IS had gone to school for special training; clients didn't have that training.

Given this environment in which the beliefs were created, they made perfect sense. Almost anyone would have reached the same conclusions if this were what they observed in the world. But is the world the same today? When asked this question, IS staffers will describe the environment in which they are operating today:

- Most of their clients know what they need.

- PCs are used for all business purposes; as part of a network they do the work of mainframes in many cases.

- There are a great many off-the-shelf software packages.

- There are many contract programmers.

- Clients' needs change daily; solutions become out of date quickly.

- Most IS clients know a lot about computers.

- Most clients have one at home.

If the IS department's behavior is a function of its beliefs and if the beliefs are the inevitable result of the older environment in which they were created, and if today's environment is drastically different, should it be doing the same thing and believing the same thing as it used to? Obviously not. But as long as the old cultural beliefs remain, there is little chance that people will be open to really looking at the new environment.

Once it becomes clear that the beliefs that run your company or department are not "*the* truth" but "*a* truth" that was valid only at the time the beliefs were created, they disappear as beliefs. That enables employees to repeat the original process: Look at the environment today, interpret it, and form not "*the* truth" but "*a* truth," which will manifest as the appropriate behavior—for today.

Day-to-Day Business Applications of TLM

Shortly after I completed workshops for one manufacturing client, many of the employees started making suggestions for improvements in the company's P's and S's. Supervisors were allowing workers to make more and more decisions on their own.

A lot of excitement was generated; many of the changes workers suggested were instituted.

Bob, the manager of a department of about thirty-five workers, went on vacation for a week. Two days after he left, Jean, one of the supervisors, handled something that everyone had agreed would be done by the workers. When Rick, one of the workers, complained to her, Jean said, in effect, "So what? I'm still the supervisor." When Rick continued to protest, Jean took him to the operations manager's office.

The other workers observed the altercation and most of them concluded, **"We're back where we started. Nothing has really changed. If you speak up you get into trouble."**

The next week Bob returned from vacation to discover that morale and productivity had sunk to a new low, with virtually no suggestions or worker participation.

What would most managers do in a situation like this? Talk to the supervisor involved in the altercation? Yes, but that in itself would have little effect on the other thirty-some workers. Talk to the workers individually and as a group, telling them that one incident isn't really important and that the new era of openness and involvement will continue? Yes, but through what filter will anything the manager says be heard by the workers? "I hear what you're saying, but you weren't here last week, and you didn't see with your own eyes as I did that **"We're back where we started. Nothing has really changed. If you speak up you get into trouble."**

Here's what Bob actually did. He called a meeting of the department's entire workforce and asked that someone explain exactly what happened while he was away. One of the workers described the incident between Jean and Rick. Bob thanked him and replied, "So most of you have concluded **We're back where we started. Nothing has really changed. If you speak up you get into trouble.** Right?"

A scattering of "Yeahs" could be heard.

Bob continued. "That's a reasonable conclusion, based on what happened between Jean and Rick. I might have concluded the same thing had I been here. Right now, however, I'd like you to play a little game with me. It's called Possibilities. I'd like you to tell me at least five or six other things that last week's incident could possibly mean. I'm not trying to invalidate your conclusion, which is as good as any other we'll find. I'd just like you to tell me what other interpretations might be possible."

After a few minutes the answers started coming from the floor.

- It could mean that Jean hasn't bought into our empowerment program, but all the other supervisors have.

- It could mean that Jean has it in for Rick, but she wouldn't be a problem for any other worker.

- It could mean that Jean was having a bad day, and she is as committed to the new empowerment program as anyone.

- It could mean that Jean is willing to delegate most of her work except for the job involved in last week's problem.

After several more responses, Bob said, "Can you see that what most of you concluded—**We're back where we started. Nothing has really changed. If you speak up you get into trouble**—is one valid interpretation of what happened, but that a number of other explanations are just as valid?"

Heads started nodding up and down.

He continued. "Didn't it seem last week when Jean and Larry were arguing that you could see right here on the factory floor **We're back where we started. Nothing has really changed. If you speak up you get into trouble**?"

One worker yelled out, "If you had been here, Bob, you'd have seen it too!"

Bob smiled. "Did you really see that? If you did, I'd like to know, was it on the wall or the floor? Was it red or green, striped or polka-dotted? Big or small? Or did you just see Rick and Jean arguing, and the only place **We're back where we started.**

Nothing has really changed. If you speak up you get into trouble has ever been is in your mind, as an interpretation of what you really did see?"

They got the point.

Bob turned to Rick. "By the way, what happened when you went to the operations manager's office with Jean?"

"He told us to work it out ourselves," Rick answered.

Bob turned back to the group. "Anything else?" He saw a lot of sheepish grins. "Let's go to work."

In most companies, hardly a day goes by that some employees don't observe something and then reach a conclusion that negatively affects their behavior. Usually their manager will try to change their behavior using Information + Motivation. That rarely works. Sometimes if the belief surfaces—**So-and-so can't be trusted** or **That new plan will never work**—TLM (or a variation) can be used easily, with one employee at a time or with a large group, just as Bob did.

How to Create a Third Order Organization

Are you beginning to get a sense of the remarkable impact TLM and its many applications can make in the daily operations of companies? You can change how individual workers see their jobs. You can change the purpose and behavior of entire departments. You can change the thinking and actions of individuals or groups of workers. And, perhaps most importantly, you can create a Third Order organization. Now let's examine five specific steps required to create a Third Order organization.

Step One: Create an Effective Mission and Operate Out of It Consistently

An organization's mission is what the organization stands for, its purpose, and its direction. Because an organization's mission is its most fundamental belief system, the mission has the potential to be its most influential belief. It rarely is, but it can be.

To be truly effective, a mission must serve as the standard for all of an organization's decisions. Every meeting should start with a reference to the mission: How is what we're about to discuss going to further the mission? If what we're about to discuss has no relevance to the mission, why are we wasting time discussing it?

The standard for each individual worker should be: What procedures, systems, policies, and practices (P's and S's) are inhibiting me from furthering the mission? Can they be eliminated totally, or can they be replaced with something that will support me rather than hinder me? Using the mission as the standard for all changes prevents workers from going off in different directions or making changes that they personally favor, but which have no direct benefit to the organization.

Step Two: Employees Change Their Beliefs about Their Jobs

As long as workers believe their job is to do the best they can, given the existing culture, and managers believe their job is to figure out what workers should do and then get them to do it, no one will take responsibility for changing the culture—much less for creating Third Order Change.

Remember, to create a Third Order Change organization:

1. Managers need to believe that their job is to create an environment in which workers do the thinking that they, the managers, used to do—and then to support workers in making the changes they propose.

2. Workers need to believe that their most important job is to figure out what P's and S's are getting in the way of them doing their jobs—and then to eliminate them.

Step Three: Don't Just Fix Problems, Eliminate Their Source

In other words, don't fix the culture you have; eliminate it and create a new one that's appropriate for today. Then keep changing it as required. The source of a continuing barrier to the mission or of any other ongoing business problem is almost always the way the culture manifests itself through its P's and S's. Most organizations solve problems by trying to "get through" them, but if all you do is fix a problem—that is, deal with it today—whatever is responsible for producing the problem will continue to produce it. You'll have to solve it repeatedly as it continues to come up.

Everyone in the company should focus on creating an effective culture, not merely on somehow getting through the existing culture, because just getting along results in less time spent creating value for the customers.

Step Four: Start Employees on Eliminating Barriers to Implementing the Mission

Usually when the executives of a company decide to make changes, they assign other executives to task forces. First, they are given the job of identifying the specific areas to be changed. They are then asked to recommend changes. There are several drawbacks to this approach. First, the executives assigned to the task force rarely have the same problems as the people whose problems they are trying to solve. Second, the executives don't have the time to undertake this assignment. Third, the solutions they come up with usually produce new problems, often as bad as the original problem they were trying to solve.

Here's an alternative approach. Who generally knows a worker's barriers better than anyone else? Who knows better what it would take to eliminate those barriers? The worker doing the job. (If your answer is "management," you haven't been reading the articles in the business press about changes made by hourly workers that are improving productivity and quality, reducing backlogs, reducing waste, and increasing customer satisfaction by 30 to 70 percent annually.)

Ask each worker if the existing culture and its P's and S's are a support or a hindrance in furthering the mission. Because they were created years earlier for a different environment, they almost always will hinder employees to some extent.

Next, starting from the top down, have each manager ask the workers to commit to changing one specific barrier (one of the P's and S's) that gets in the way of implementing the mission. After they make their commitment, those managers should ask the next level, and so forth, until every employee in the company has made a commitment.

It won't be particularly difficult to get most people to identify a barrier to their implementing the mission and then commit to eliminating it. In many cases, a large number of people will not do what they commit to. The actual response will resemble a bell-shaped curve: The 20 percent on one side will be excited and thinking of what to change and how to change it before you leave them. The 20 percent on the other side will think that the entire process is nonsense, that things are okay the way they are, and that if any change is needed it's minor. This group will resist and even possibly try to sabotage the process. The remaining 60 percent in the middle will like the idea of creating a Third Order organization, but will be very skeptical and cynical. They will not believe that significant change really will happen, and they think they have a lot of evidence for that belief.

Most people who want to create major organizational change, when confronted with this 20-60-20 percent ratio, would decide to ignore the 20 percent who oppose the whole idea of a Third Order organization and also the 20 percent who are eager to start looking for what to change. They would focus on trying to convince the skeptical 60 percent who are watching and waiting. But why aren't the 60 percent who support the idea of Third Order Change acting? Because they think they saw with their eyes that no one is interested in their ideas and that significant change never will happen.

You could, theoretically, do TLM with every one of the 60 percent and eliminate that belief. Apart from the fact that many would refuse to do TLM with you, this approach would be difficult and time-consuming. So here's an alternative method. Focus on the 20 percent who are going to act. My experience in a number of organizations that have tried this, and the experience of various "cultures" that have made significant changes (for example, farmers using new hybrid seeds or equipment and natives using boiled water), shows that if the first 20 percent succeed, the rest will follow. If they don't, the rest never do. Management must first make sure that the suggestions received from the initial 20 percent get implemented, and then it must publicize the changes to the other 60 percent so that they can repeatedly see with their eyes that employees' suggestions are really being used and that all employees really have been empowered to make changes.[9] If management does this, some of the 60 percent who are watching will start saying, "Hey, what they said really was true. There is a commitment to make fundamental changes. Maybe they will listen to me now."

A few months later, the proportion of those who watch vs. those who act will shift from 60—20, to 50—30, then 40—40, and so on. In less time than you would expect, there is sufficient momentum to sustain the process of convincing additional employees to make fundamental changes. Within a year or so there is a visible shift in the culture.

Step Five: When Employees Focus on Solutions, Management Can't Say No

Make a rule that employees are not allowed to bring in problems, only solutions. And remember, by solution I don't mean a "First Order fix" but a Third Order Change in the culture, such as new policies, procedures, and systems that will eliminate the source of a problem.

Then, if an employee suggests a way to change some P's and S's that are barriers to implementing the mission, and if the suggested change does not adversely affect any other employee, management is not allowed to say "No, we won't change the way we do things around here."[10]

When the people who have to do the job of implementing the company's strategy and mission submit a proposed change, they are saying that the culture is getting in their way. Management might have to work with them to modify their proposals so that no one else in the organization is hindered by the proposed change, but management can never tell anyone that they have to accept the existing culture if it is a barrier to implementing the organization's mission. (At this point the importance of an effective mission statement becomes even clearer.) Within a relatively short period of time, the company will not only have made significant changes in its culture, so that operations have become more consistent with the mission and the current environment, something even more important will have happened.

If you were to ask employees in any company today, "Who is responsible for fixing what doesn't work for you?" Who would they name? Probably someone other than themselves. But after they and 80 percent of their fellow employees have made the changes they want to make, to whom will they turn to eliminate the next barrier to the mission that they identify? The very ones who identified and eliminated the last barrier—themselves! A company where this occurred on a regular basis would be a Third Order organization.[11] Third Order organizations will resolve one of society's biggest problems- the apparent conflict between companies that pursue profits and companies that care about employees. Third Order organizations achieve their financial success by giving employees what they really want from a job—the chance to really make a difference.

Chapter 11

Making Society Work

*The United States is in the midst of a great
transformation, comparable to the one that ended
medievalism and shook its institutions to the ground. ... .
The old ideas and assumptions that once made our
institutions legitimate are being eroded. They are
slipping away in the face of a changing reality, being
replaced by different ideas as yet ill-formed,
contradictory, unsettling.*

—George Cabot Lodge

*A*s *far back* as I can remember, I had the sense that society
didn't work. There was too much pain, suffering, and unhappiness.
Too many people got left out. Even as a child, the distinction
between the "haves" and the "have-nots" was obvious to me. It was
so unfair. Because I considered myself to be a "have-not," I
decided that the way to deal with a dangerous world was to place
myself in a position where it couldn't touch me or hurt me. I
created a survival strategy belief: **The way to survive in life is to
have a lot of money and make friends with important people
who can help me if I get in trouble.** In other words, to escape the
danger, I must become one of the "haves." (Because I also formed
beliefs like **I'll never get what I want** and **I'm not deserving**, I
was unable to succeed with my survival strategy. The result: a lot
of anxiety and depression for many years.)

After I took the est training, however, my focus shifted. At
that point, rather than insulating myself from a hostile world, I

became committed to improving it. I continually saw people make significant, positive changes in their lives after they took the est training. By working for est, both as a paid employee and as a volunteer seminar leader and training supervisor, I experienced a great deal of satisfaction in knowing that I was making a valuable contribution to the lives of thousands of people.

Most of all, it was my work assisting Werner Erhard to create The Hunger Project (THP) that first gave me a sense that change was possible on a much grander scale—that entire areas of life or institutions of society could be changed and improved. I helped prepare the initial Hunger Project presentations that were made to about 35,000 people in 1977, and then I helped Werner edit THP's Source Document. It was during the time I worked on this position paper that I first clearly realized how beliefs could make it impossible to solve a social problem such as global hunger.

Growing up, I saw the failure of repeated attempts to solve problems in every area of life, including welfare, crime, the environment, foreign policy, child abuse, prejudice against women, racism, and health care. Several years after I developed TLM (early 1985), I finally understood why most of the attempts failed: In virtually every area, the existing paradigms—the collections of beliefs related to a specific aspect of life—were no longer appropriate to today's circumstances. As a result, one of two things happened. Either the attempted solutions were not effective in dealing with the problems, because they were consistent with the existing inappropriate paradigm, or the strategies were potentially useful but widespread implementation was impossible because the strategies were inconsistent with the existing paradigm of the institution.

This realization propelled me to begin examining institutions and their collective beliefs to find ways that TLM could be used to change institutional paradigms so that workable solutions could be devised and implemented relatively easily. Once you understand the power that beliefs have to shape behavior and limit possibilities, you can see why so many of society's problems seem insoluble. It suddenly makes sense why every proposed solution in health care, crime, education, and foreign policy has so many negative aspects, and why no one can seem to find a solution that doesn't have as many negatives as positives. We've tried virtually every option in the old boxes, and the problems continue to grow worse.

As I described in chapter 10, the focus of my work with organizations is on assisting employees to create a "meta-culture" that facilitates change. My role is to provide them with TLM, which enables them to make changes. Specifically, they learn how to create a Third Order organization in which each employee assumes responsibility for figuring out what needs to be done to implement the company's mission. Once they learn how to use TLM, *they* decide—not I—which aspects of the culture they want to change and what they want the change to look like.

The same is true for people concerned with their professions and institutions. This chapter is designed to provide people who are trying to make fundamental improvements in institutions like the health care system and education with a technology that will enable them to succeed. TLM Technology will enable them to understand (1) why change has been so difficult and (2) how to get people to let go of the existing paradigm and be open to adopting a new one. Then a new group of beliefs and viable strategies that are consistent with it can be adopted.

The purpose of this chapter is not to provide alternative beliefs or the intricate details of various solutions. My intention here is to make clear why the existing paradigms keep most attempts to improve our institutions from succeeding, and how TLM can be used to change these institutional paradigms so workable solutions can be devised and implemented.

I will provide a few illustrations of what alternative paradigms and strategies could look like in the areas of education and health care. But I won't spend a lot of time on my alternatives because I'm not pushing them. In my experience, the people who work in organizations and institutions are the best source of solutions—once new beliefs have been created.

TLM explains why there are no workable solutions in the existing boxes—the current paradigms. It enables us to realize that the problems we face today in virtually every area of life cannot be solved with the options that exist. Ultimately, what we need is a society that practices "TLM thinking." The result would be a profound realization that "*the* truth" about education, health care, or any other institution does not exist. What is needed is "*a* (new) truth" that is more appropriate for the moment—and should be replaced when future conditions require it.

The Folly of Our Beliefs

If you need an example of the way anachronistic beliefs have stood in the way of workable solutions to institutional problems, you need only look at our educational system. Few institutional arenas are subject to as much passion, dissent, and, ultimately, paralysis as education. The modified version of TLM used in organizations shows why we are so deadlocked—and how that deadlock might be transcended.

Most people agree that there is a problem with education in this country. And a great many believe that the problem can be solved at least partially by instituting national standards.

Why does a fixed plan for educational improvement—the idea of setting measurable standards and goals—appeal to so many people? I suspect it is because of the belief **There is a certain amount of information that should be learned in school.** Thus, **Setting up national standards is a very good way to insure that.**

Where did we, as a society, initially get that idea? To answer, we must go back in time.

When compulsory education was initiated in America over a century ago, its purpose was to prepare people to work in factories. Workers needed to read and write and be able to follow instructions. What a person knew about the world remained true during a lifetime of forty some years. The amount of new knowledge produced during adult life was minimal. It wasn't particularly important that one learn how to think independently or creatively. Given such an environment, it made sense to conclude that there was a certain amount of information needed to succeed in life and that the function of school was to provide that information. The belief about the importance of learning a certain amount of information while in school was not wrong when it was formed. It made perfect sense and was totally appropriate, given the circumstances. It was the logical outcome of looking at the world as it existed in that historical moment in time.

In today's world, however, "facts" are in a constant state of change. The amount of new knowledge produced every few years is greater than all the accumulated knowledge to date. The ability to succeed in the business world today (forget succeed—the ability even to get hired!) depends not so much on the quantity of information you know and how well you can follow orders but on your ability to think and act on your own. As Alvin Toffler put it, "The illiterate of the future are not those that cannot read or write, but those that cannot learn, unlearn, and relearn."

Today, people are not only changing jobs several times during their work lives, many of them are changing careers several times. Moreover, it has become increasingly clear that a satisfying life consists of more than business success. It requires a good sense of yourself, the ability to relate well to others, and lots more.

The proposal for national standards to measure how much information has been learned in school is consistent with the existing paradigm, but that group of beliefs is no longer appropriate. We need schools that operate within a new educational model that's appropriate for today, one that opens the possibility for new educational strategies. There are some schools providing what is needed, but by definition they are "alternative" schools, operating outside the prevailing set of beliefs.

Let's consider the difference between the "old" set of beliefs and a possible new one that is more appropriate for our times (shown below).

Beliefs of the Old Paradigm of Education	Beliefs of One New Paradigm of Learning
It is important to emphasize facts, acquiring a body of "right information," once and for all.	It important we emphasize learning how to learn, how to ask good questions, being open to and evaluating new concepts; teaching "facts" should be secondary because much of what is now "known" may change.
Learning is a product, a destination to be reached.	Learning is a process, a journey.
The priority is performance.	The priority is on self-image as the generator of performance.
The external world is looked to for virtually all the answers.	Inner experience is the context for learning.
The emphasis is on analytical, linear, left-brained thinking.	Left-brained rationality is augmented with holistic, nonlinear, and intuitive strategies.
There is a primary reliance on theoretical, abstract "book" knowledge.	Theoretical and abstract knowledge is heavily complemented by experiment and experience, both in and out of the classroom.
Education is a social necessity for a certain period of time, to inculcate certain minimum skills and train for a specific role.	Education is a lifelong process, one only tangentially related to schools.
Teachers impart knowledge; education is a one-way street.	Teachers are learners too, learning from students.

Adapted from: Marilyn Ferguson, *The Aquarian Conspiracy*. Los Angeles: J. P. Tarcher, 1980

Notice that the beliefs constituting the existing paradigm generate questions and strategies about how to achieve norms, obedience, and correct answers. The new beliefs lead to questions and strategies about how to motivate for lifelong learning, how to strengthen self-discipline, how to awaken curiosity, and how to encourage creative risk-taking in people of all ages.

Ron Miller, author of *What Are Schools For?* describes the essence of this new paradigm:

> Holistic educators recognize that all aspects of life are interconnected. They contend that education must be concerned with the physical, emotional, social, aesthetic/creative, and spiritual qualities of every person, as well as traditionally emphasized intellectual and vocational skills. . . . In our culture, "education" is implicitly equated with the transmission of information, particularly through written sources. But holistic educators have, for two centuries, asserted that education is *an active engagement between a person and a vastly complex world*. Holistic education emphasizes experience, not "Great Books" or a few "basic skills.". . . Why limit students to a curriculum of academic subjects when the entire cosmos is at hand? Education, as John Dewey so eloquently argued, must not be seen as "preparation" for life—it *is* life! Education is growth, discovery, and a widening of horizons. This is just the opposite of traditional educational goals—discipline, order, high test scores—that aim to prepare children for the limited world which the adult generation has created.[1]

If this description of an alternative model for education is a possible one for today's circumstances, what strategies might we use to improve the educational system? We might focus on learning how to ask the right questions and how to think, rather than on dry facts that are not seen as relevant to one's life. We might give students more responsibility for their own learning. We might use more learning experiences outside the classroom. We might relate the information that is taught to each student's daily life. We might blend information from different areas together into core curricula so that students learn math when they study art and grammar when they study drama.

Strategies already exist that could solve most of today's educational problems.[2] What is missing is a paradigm that allows them. Where workable strategies do not already exist, people with knowledge and an interest in education could create them, as long as they are operating from a new group of beliefs.[3]

Creating a New Paradigm

You are now beginning to see how the roots of our institutional problems lie in the beliefs that comprise our institutional paradigms, and not in the quality of our solutions. What is the process by which we might eliminate an existing paradigm and create a new one?

Let's use the health care system—another paralyzing institutional problem—to show how our reliance on "*the* [old] truth" is limiting our possibilities for viable solutions. The following process, based on TLM, can be used to escape from the confines of the existing paradigm so that a new one, appropriate for today, can be created.

Step One: State the Problem

Virtually everyone agrees that the existing health care system doesn't work, even though there are a number of conflicting theories about why and what should be done. What's wrong? Insurance premiums are rising faster than the ability of millions of people to pay. Tens of millions of people aren't covered by any insurance at all. An increasing percentage of our national income is being spent on medical care. People with preexisting conditions can't get insurance. People who can't pay aren't getting the medical treatment they need.

Step Two: Examine the Strategies Presented as Solutions

Suggested approaches to deal with these problems include price controls on medical services, managed competition (in all its variations), HMOs, PPOs, a government-subsidized system like Canada's, increasing the deductible amount, having employees pay a larger share of the premium, having the insured pay a larger percentage and the insurance company a smaller percentage of the bill, having business pay the full cost of insuring all employees, and having the government reimburse employers.

Every proposal has serious drawbacks. If business pays all the costs, companies will have to raise prices and lay off employees. HMOs can reduce costs, but the patients are limited in their choices of doctors, and a lot of valuable treatment may be excluded. In HMOs, physicians are frequently encouraged to practice "cost-effective" medicine, which isn't always the best medical care. If insurance companies are forced to insure everyone and allow policyholders to get whatever treatment they want, premiums will increase even higher and faster. If the government pays all medical bills, the federal deficit will continue to increase.

Step Three: Identify the Underlying Beliefs

After years of trying many of these alternatives, which either have made no noticeable improvement or have created almost as many problems as they solved, it should be clear that a truly workable option—quality health care available to everyone at an affordable price—doesn't exist in the current paradigm. We've been looking in the wrong place for a solution. What is required is a new model that will create fresh, heretofore unimaginable options.

Virtually all legislation that has been considered during the past few years exists in the current paradigm. What is this paradigm? What current beliefs govern all proposed strategies?

- Health care should focus on eliminating symptoms and disease.

- Body and mind are considered separate; psychosomatic illness is mental and may be referred to a psychiatrist. Mental phenomena are irrelevant in treating most physical illnesses.

- The body is a machine in good or bad repair. The primary intervention should be with drugs and surgery.

- The focus should be on treatment of symptoms.

- There should be a high degree of specialization.

- The patient is dependent. The professional is the authority.

Step Four: Find the Source of the Beliefs

Descartes, the seventeenth-century French philosopher, taught that everything in the material universe was a machine, including human beings. He claimed that the human body reflected the machinelike characteristics of the universe itself—machinelike bodies inhabiting a machinelike world.[4] He argued, therefore, that disease was a disorder of the mechanism; the machine was broken. Descartes devised what became known as the scientific or reductionist method: To learn about the complex, study the simple. Learn about a germ, and eventually you learn about the disease associated with it.

A medical theory that supported Descartes's general scientific approach was the theory of specific etiology: Every disease or infection is caused by an identifiable microorganism.

In their book *The Healer Within*, Steven Locke and Norman Coligan describe the medical advances that flowed from these two theories:

In 1906 researchers used Koch's discovery of the tuberculin bacillus to develop a vaccine for the disease. In 1911 researchers developed a special arsenic compound, Salvarsan, that effectively treated many forms of syphilis. In the 1920s insulin was isolated, and insulin injections were extending the lifetimes of diabetic patients. In the 1930s, sulfa drugs appeared, and with them cures for bacterial pneumonia, meningitis, gonorrhea, and urinary tract infections. By the 1940s, the sulfa drugs were largely replaced by even more potent drugs, the antibiotics, made possible by the discovery of penicillin. It seemed that there was no disease that medical science could not handle.[5]

So where did physicians (and their patients) get the belief that the source of most illness and disease was an invading microorganism or a malfunction of the body/machine and that the influence of the mind was irrelevant? From their experience over several decades. As Locke and Colligan put it, "For most of the history of modern medicine this biomedical approach has dominated the philosophy of science for the best of all reasons: it worked." The biomedical approach resulted in physicians focusing more on diseases than on the patients who had the diseases. This trend was exacerbated by advances in medical technology, an early example of which was the stethoscope in 1319. Locke and Colligan write that diagnostic technologies:

> Further reinforced the image of the patient as an object of study. By the turn of the century, doctors had tests for tuberculosis, diphtheria, typhoid, cholera, and syphilis. Soon after came the X-ray, the electrocardiogram, the electroencephalogram, and blood tests. The patient became less and less a fellow human being with an illness and more and more an amalgam of medical data.[6]

So where did physicians (and their patients) get the idea that a doctor's job was to diagnose an illness and treat it, as opposed to dealing with a whole person who had a body and a mind? Again, from their experience in dealing with the world. Their conclusion was not illogical or invalid. It made sense. Their interpretation fit most of the available evidence. The problem was that the medical establishment considered this conclusion an absolute fact— "*the* truth" rather than "*a* truth"—the only accurate description of illness and how the body worked, then and forever. Once the belief was formed, they became blinded to new evidence that was incompatible with their beliefs.[7]

Step Five: Observe Today's Environment

We are increasingly gathering evidence of a mind-body connection in the cause and treatment of illness—as we discussed in chapter 8. For example, according to some physicians, the power of hypnosis to affect the body makes it a promising tool for treating burn victims; Dabney Edwin, professor of surgery and psychiatric at Tulane University, has been using hypnosis to treat severe cases. Dr. Edwin has found that hypnotizing a patient within hours of an injury has had significant effects on the speed and completeness of recovery. Other physicians using hypnosis have had similar results.

If there is no mind-body connection, how can the healing process be dramatically improved by nothing more than a belief that the part of the body that has been burned is "beginning to feel cool and comfortable"? If a change in your mental state can change your EEG patterns, blood pressure, skin conditions, and even eye color—something medical scientists have assumed is totally determined by your genes—is it difficult to imagine that a belief such as **I'm unworthy** could contribute to producing illness?

There are many tangible examples in medical practice of the mind-body connection. One of the best proofs that beliefs have a powerful impact on our health has existed for years right under the noses of every physician in the world: the placebo effect, "a change in a patient's illness attributable to the symbolic import of a treatment rather than a specific pharmacologic or physiological property." In other words, it is your natural healing ability triggered by belief in a treatment, doctor, or institution.

Every new drug is tested for safety and efficacy before it is put on the market. Part of all testing involves giving the drug to human subjects to determine if it is effective in dealing with the condition it's intended to alleviate. At the same time, a pill containing an inert substance, sometimes sugar, is given to other subjects with the same illness. The drug is approved for distribution if it is determined to be safe and significantly more effective than the placebo. As Deepak Chopra points out:

> By giving a placebo, or dummy pill, thirty percent of patients will experience the same pain relief as if a real painkiller had been administered. But the mind-body effect is much more holistic. The same dummy pill can be used to kill pain, to stop excessive gastric secretions in ulcer patients, to lower blood pressure, or to fight tumors. (All the side effects of chemotherapy, including hair loss and nausea, can be induced by giving cancer patients a sugar pill while assuring them that it is a powerful anticancer drug, and there have been instances where injections of sterile saline solution have actually led to remissions of advanced malignancy.)[8]

An excellent example of the mind-body connection is cancer. The old saying, "Many a truth has been spoken in jest" was never more true than when Woody Allen said in the film *Manhattan*, "I don't get mad, I grow tumors." Cancer is a disease caused by a failure of the immune system. What causes the immune system to fail in some people and not in others? Increasingly, scientists and cancer specialists are reaching the same conclusion Norman Cousins wrote about in *Head First*. Cousins summarized research showing that depression is a demonstrated cause of physical ill health, including deleterious effects on the immune system. Equally striking is the fact that liberation from depression produces an almost automatic boost in the number of disease-fighting immune cells. Cousins concluded, "If you can reduce the depression that almost invariably affects cancer patients, you can increase the body's own capacity for combating malignancies."[9]

Depression is experienced as an overwhelming sense of hopelessness and helplessness. Those attitudes are the result of such beliefs as **I'm not good enough, I don't matter, I'll never get what I want, People can't be trusted, Life is difficult,** and

I'm not safe in the world. By eliminating beliefs such as these, depression can be eliminated and the immune system can be strengthened.[10]

Another example of the mind-body connection is heart disease. Scientists have long been puzzled by the fact that, although the "risk factors" for heart disease (like high blood cholesterol, diabetes, high blood pressure, and cigarette smoking) are well known, more than half the new cases of heart disease occur when none of these risk factors is present. Something else is going on. Scientists have also learned that the most reliable factor in determining survival rates for patients with heart disease are job satisfaction and a sense of "overall happiness." Those who were alone and depressed had the poorest survival rates. Lynda H. Powell, an assistant professor at the Department of Epidemiology and Public Health at the Yale University School of Medicine, has done extensive research on the relationship between mental states and heart attacks. Dr. Powell points out:

> Hostility and cynical mistrust are consistently associated with coronary artery disease. The constant ongoing vigilance associated with being mistrustful appears to promote coronary heart disease by speeding up the disposition on the atherosclerotic plaques on the walls of the arteries. How we think this happens is that the hormones which enter the bloodstream during times of stress act to keep the sticky LDL cholesterol, which is considered the bad type of cholesterol, circulating in the bloodstream longer, and this increases the rate of blockage on the coronary arteries.[11]

It is clear that we now live in a world that is very different from the one we inhabited a century ago, a world in which there is irrefutable scientific evidence of a mind-body connection, evidence that existed only anecdotally during the years that the paradigm for modern medicine was being created.[12] The current paradigm is at variance with the new medical reality, as Larry Dossey points out:

What is the success of modern medicine? What *can* it do? These are the questions in need of answers in the debate. . . . The fact is that for the majority of patients who see physicians, the likeliest diagnosis is some type of psychosomatic or stress disorder. And regrettably, it is in this area—the area from which most patients suffer—that modern medicine is not at its best. . . Actual studies show that three-fourths of all illnesses brought to physicians are self-limiting (that is, will go away without medical treatment). And of the remaining one-fourth, in only about half of the cases is medicine dramatically helpful.[13]

None of this is meant to denigrate physicians or modern medicine. The only point I'm making here is that what we observe when we look at what is known about health and illness today is vastly different from what we observed a century or so ago when the current medical model was being formed.

Step Six: Create a Paradigm for Today

Today's strategies are a function of an institution's group of beliefs, which in turn was designed to be an appropriate response to a specific environment that existed when it was created. If today's environment is significantly different, can you see that neither the current strategies nor the paradigm can work for today? That neither are "the truth"? It's fitting to ask: If we originally devised a successful paradigm and a course of action that was based on a careful analysis of the environment as it existed then, why don't we do the same today?

Contrast one new paradigm of health with the current paradigm (shown below).

Beliefs of the Old Paradigm of Medicine	Beliefs of One New Paradigm of Health
Emphasis on eliminating symptoms.	Emphasis on achieving maximum wellness, "meta-health."
Body and mind are separate; psychosomatic illness is mental, may be referred to a psychiatrist.	Body-mind perspective; psychosomatic illness is the province of all health care professionals.
Body seen as machine in good and bad repair.	Body seen as dynamic system, field of energy within other fields.
Primary intervention with drugs, surgery.	Minimal intervention with "appropriate technology" complemented with full armamentarium of noninvasive techniques (psychotherapies, diet, exercise).
Treatment of symptoms.	Search for patterns and causes, plus treatment of symptoms.
Specialized.	Integrated, concerned with the whole patient.
Disease or disability seen as thing, entity.	Disease or disability seen as process.
Patient is dependent.	Patient is autonomous.
Professional is authority.	Professional is therapeutic partner.
Primary reliance on quantitative information (charts, tests, dates).	Primary reliance on qualitative information, including patient's subjective reports and professional's intuition; quantitative data an adjunct.
Mind is secondary factor in organic illness.	Mind is primary or equal factor in all illness.
"Prevention" largely environmental; vitamins, rest, exercise, immunization, not smoking.	"Prevention" synonymous with wholeness: work, relationships, goals, body-mind-spirit.

Adapted from: Marilyn Ferguson, *The Aquarian conspiracy*. Los Angeles: J. P. Tarcher. 1980

Notice that for the most part the existing beliefs generate questions and strategies about illness, especially how professionals can make people better after they get sick, usually using such "mechanical" aids as drugs or surgery. Can you see that the beliefs constituting one possible new paradigm lead to questions and strategies about a state of wellness, emphasizing prevention, involving the patient as well as the professional, and using the patient's internal resources as a significant aid?

Step Seven: Create Strategies Consistent with the New Paradigm to Solve Existing Problems

If people trying to solve the health care problem sought solutions consistent with the alternative paradigm just suggested, and if everyone involved in the process viewed potential solutions from this alternative paradigm, it wouldn't be long before alternative solutions were devised, accepted, and implemented. Each belief that constitutes a new paradigm opens up new possibilities for strategies and solutions. Experts in each field can provide better solutions than I can, and many have already. What's been missing is the acceptance of a paradigm that allows solutions outside the existing one. Once people realize that the existing paradigm is "*a* truth," not "*the* truth," and view the alternative paradigm presented here as another "*a* truth," one that is more appropriate for today, new health care and wellness strategies will be devised and implemented.[14] Perpetuating an outdated paradigm makes it impossible to resolve the problems of society. As Scaborn Blair once said, "Everybody wants to change the world, but nobody wants to change his mind." Why don't we want to change our minds? Because we are convinced that our beliefs are "the truth."

Our only hope for resolving the myriad problems that confront us today and really improving the state of the world is to change our minds. If we are to create a society that really works for everyone, we must get unstuck from our existing beliefs and open our minds to alternative ones. TLM can enable people to do just that. It can be used to eliminate the outmoded paradigms that prevent us from finding viable solutions to today's problems. TLM is one excellent tool for easing the way for a "Third Wave" information/knowledge society to come into being—along with transformed institutions and a more holistic and spiritual approach to life.

<u>Epilogue</u>

Unlimited Possibilities

*The future is not some place we are
going to, but a place we are creating.*
—John Schaar

I*n a recent* business workshop, just as I finished
explaining the relationship between beliefs and behavior, one of the
participants suddenly exclaimed, "This is crazy!" I stopped talking
and looked at him curiously. "What is?" I wondered what I had
said to make him disagree so violently. His answer was totally
unexpected. "Why didn't we learn this in grammar school? Why I
am finding this out now at the age of forty?" I grinned at him.
"Better late than never." Then, assuming a more serious tone, I said,
"I am committed to seeing that in the future people won't have to
wait as long as you did—or have to ask that question."

The Ever-Open Possibility

That is my commitment: To get TLM out into the world.
Not because I think I have all the answers. Nothing in this book is
"*the* truth." The ideas expressed here are only one way of looking
at life. Yet, it is one that appears to empower us to make
fundamental and needed changes—in ourselves, in our
organizations, and in our institutions. There are other ways of
looking at life that are just as valid, but I don't know any that are as
empowering—that enable us to get unstuck from our current
dysfunctional patterns and create new possibilities in life. I am not
pushing a specific point of view. This book, unlike most books that

give advice on how to change, is not about First, or even Second Order Change. It is about Third Order Change. I'm not even saying that existing societal paradigms are wrong and another one is right. I'm saying there aren't any paradigms that are "*the* truth." There are only belief systems that work and those that don't work, given particular circumstances at a particular time. Today, most of our paradigms don't work, at least if our standards are peace and respect for people of different genders, skin colors, sexual preferences, and religious faiths. They don't work if we long for a sense that nothing is missing: Inner satisfaction, relationships that nurture us, organizations that empower us, and institutions that truly support us.

The Power of TLM Thinking

The radically different type of thinking that TLM proposes is really the essence of creativity. It is the ability to view the world from outside the boxes most people live in. As William James observed, "Genius, in truth, means little more than the faculty of perceiving in an unhabitual way." Thinking that assumes there is no "the truth," that constantly creates new possibilities, that enables you to perceive "in an unhabitual way," is TLM thinking. But in order to think that way—in order to be willing to give up beliefs you've known as "*the* truth" and live out of questions rather than answers—you need to realize that all meaning is an interpretation that you make.

We are empowered when we can create new possibilities, thus, mastering TLM thinking is the ultimate empowerment. It also is a revolution in thinking.

I expect this book will spawn thousands of formal and informal research projects on how best to use TLM in every area of life. I want to encourage people to use TLM thinking to create a Third Order society. I hope millions of people use TLM to transform their organizations and institutions. I intend that even more people learn how to use TLM to help others make changes in their lives.

The Mission of The Lefkoe Institute

The mission of The Lefkoe Institute is: "To facilitate people to live, not only as the creation they normally experience themselves to be, but also as the creator of that creation—by enabling them to discover that their personal, organizational, institutional, and societal beliefs are not 'the truth' but only 'a truth' they created—so that each and every one of us experiences serenity, satisfaction, nothing missing, no limitations, and unlimited possibilities, individually and in relationships with each other."

I think that TLM is urgently needed. If you consider what you normally do when you're upset or need advice, your options are woefully inadequate. It should be possible to have someone always available to facilitate you in the LBP so you can discover the beliefs that are producing any given problem as it arises and then eliminate them. There ought to be millions of people who can use TLM with others, such as friends, teachers, parents, facilitators available at the office, or professionals available to help anyone who drops in for a session. I am training TLM facilitators as quickly as I can, so they can help people deal with dysfunctional patterns they can't handle on their own or with the assistance of a friend.

Participating in a LBP session, however, is not about fixing your life once and for all. It's about growth. It's about constantly creating new possibilities for your life. It's about experiencing life as a game, one in which you create more and more possibilities and fewer and fewer restrictions. It's about making the space of the creator real for yourself all the time.

You created your life just the way it is. To be more precise, you created the beliefs that have resulted in your life being the way it is today—even if you haven't been aware of it. And even if you have, it's unlikely you've had the ability to actually eliminate your beliefs. That's exactly the situation I was in on January 2, 1985: I had finally discovered that my beliefs were responsible for what wasn't working in my life, but I didn't know how to change them. TLM offers you, as it offered me, the opportunity to re-create your life today—the way you consciously choose it to be now, instead of the way you unconsciously created it years ago.

Embrace Fundamental Change

I have written this book because I think that much of what I've learned on my journey thus far will empower you and make a profound difference in your life. In order to take advantage of the book, you must first realize the need for fundamental change and then be open to the possibility of it. If you know that it's impossible to permanently change beliefs, this book will hold little value for you.

If, however, you are willing to look at the source of your beliefs, acknowledge that there are other possible interpretations or explanations for the events you experienced, and then realize that you didn't see what you now hold as a belief, you can create unlimited possibilities.

Most of what I present in this book, including the philosophical principles that underlie TLM, is very real to people when they are facilitated in the LBP. In the non-ordinary state of consciousness that people get into when they do TLM, they experience with profound clarity: **I am the creator of my life, there's nothing missing, there are no limitations, and anything is possible.** I'm not telling you this to convince you that it is true but to report the experience my clients and I have shared. It's analogous to reporting that I climbed a mountain and discovered that water boils at a lower temperature at higher altitudes. The point of reporting that is not to convince you of what I said; it's to describe what will happen if you were to boil water at 10,000 feet. Climb to 10,000 feet and boil water and discover for yourself what temperature is required.

Have someone use the modified version of the LBP to help you eliminate a belief you know you have and discover for yourself what happens. Use it with your children or to improve your results in athletic activities. Use TLM in your organization. Use it to start transforming our institutions. Try using TLM so that you can discover the benefits you and the rest of society can derive from them.

Create Your Future

Please write me with your e-mail address if you want to be put on our mailing list. We will keep you informed about TLM workshops, further developments in TLM, blog posts, results of research studies, and so on. I especially look forward to hearing how you've used TLM to improve your life and to discuss with you how together we can use it to transform individuals and to transform our organizations and society (e-mail: morty@lefkoeinstitute.com; web-site: www.mortylefkoe.com). We've got a big job ahead of us, but as John Schaar of the University of California wrote in "The Future," one of my favorite poems:

> The future is not a result of choices
> among alternative paths offered by the present,
> but a place that is created,
> first in mind,
> next in will, then in activity.

> The future is not some place we are going to,
> but a place we are creating.

> The paths are not to be discovered, but made,
> and the activity of making the future changes
> both the maker and the destination.

Notes

Prologue: My Personal Journey

1. Despite all the negative publicity that est and Werner Erhard have received, the importance of the est training in my life is undeniable. I still consider it to be one of the most significant experiences in my life. I am able to distinguish between the value of the programs offered, the company that offers the programs (Landmark Education, the new name for the est organization), and the man who created the original organization and training. I don't think discovering that an organization or an individual has done something you condemn in itself affects the value of the programs offered.

1: Is Profound Change Possible?

1. According to the *Yup'ik Eskimo Dictionary* compiled by Steven A. Jacobson (Alaska Native Language Center, University of Alaska, 1984), what an Eskimo would mean by these four words are "light snow," "soft deep snow," "drifting snow," and "fresh snow."

2: Principles of TLM

1. Time, 17 July 1995, p. 49.
2. Benjamin Lee Whorl has written extensively on the relationship between thought and language. In his most famous book, *Language, Thought, and Reality: Selected Writings of Benjamin Lee Whorf.* ed. by John B. Carroll (Cambridge, Mass.: MIT Press, 1956), he proposes that language plays an extensive role in perception. His thesis has become known as the Whorfian hypothesis.

This book is a brilliant analysis of the relationship between language and thinking and perception, with numerous illustrations of how the Indo-European Languages (for example, English and the languages of the peoples of Europe) have created one worldview and people speaking other languages, such as Hopi,

Maya, the dialects of other Indian tribes, and Chinese, have created very different world views.

It is difficult to prove conclusively his (and my) thesis—that reality is a function of distinctions, and that language is a major instrument by which human beings make distinctions—with only a summary of his arguments. It really is necessary to study the full range of Whorl's examples and arguments to understand fully why he concludes that "the picture of the universe shifts from tongue to tongue." Nonetheless, the following quotation provides a good sense of his line of reasoning.

"We cut up and organize the spread and flow of events as we do, largely because, through our mother tongue, we are parties to an agreement to do so, not because nature itself is segmented in exactly that way for all to see. Languages differ not only in how they build their sentences, but also in how they break down nature to secure the elements to put in these sentences....By these more or less distinct terms we ascribe a semi-fictitious isolation to parts of experience. English terms, like 'sky, hill, swamp,' persuade us to regard some elusive aspect of nature's endless variety as a distinct THING, almost like a table or chair. Thus, English and similar tongues lead us to think of the universe as a collection of rather distinct objects and events corresponding to words. Indeed, this is the implicit picture of classical physics and astronomy—that the universe is essentially a collection of detached objects of different sizes."

3. Edward Sapir, *Language, Culture, and Personality: Essays in Memory of Edward Sapir*. Leslie Sapir. ed. (Menasha, Wisc.: Sapir Memorial Publications Fund, 1941).

4. A dramatic (and sobering!) example of how language determines the distinctions we make can be found in the specific technical language that is used to describe nuclear weapons and arms control. Carol Cohn, a senior research fellow at the Center for Psychological Studies in the Nuclear Age, Cambridge, Massachusetts, spent a year as a visiting scholar at a defense studies center. She published some of her experiences in the Summer 1987 issue of SIGNS: *The Journal of Women in Culture and Society*, 01987 by The University of Chicago Press, in an

article titled "Nuclear Language and How We Learned to Pat the Bomb." She wrote, in part:

> The better I became at this discourse [of arms control], the more difficult it became to express my own ideas and values. While the language included things I had never been able to speak about before, it radically excluded others. To pick a bald example, the word 'peace' is not a part of this discourse. As close as one can come to it is strategic stability, a term that refers to a balance of numbers and types of weapons systems—not the political, social, economic, and psychological conditions that 'peace' implies. . . . If I was unable to speak my concerns in this language, more disturbing still was that I also began to find it harder to keep them in my own head. No matter how firm my own commitment to staying aware of the bloody reality behind the words, over and over I found that I could not keep human lives as my reference point.... I was so involved in the military justifications for not using nuclear weapons—as though the moral ones were not enough. What I was actually talking about—the mass incineration of a nuclear attack— was no longer in my head. As I learned to speak [this new language], I no longer stood outside the impenetrable wall of technostrategic language, and once inside, I could no longer see it. I had not only learned to speak a language: *I had started to think in it. Its questions became my questions, its concepts shaped my responses to new ideas.* (emphasis added).

5. Ralph Strauch. *The Reality Illusion: How We Create the World We Experience* (Wheaton, IlL: Theosophical Publishing House, 1982), pp. 39-40.

6. Larry Dossey, *Space. Time, and Medicine* (Boston: Shambhala, 1985), p. 203.

7. Lawrence LeShan, *Alternate Realities: The Search for the Full Human Being* (New York: M. Evans & Co., 1976), p.6.

8. Christopher Cerf and Victor Navasky. *The Experts Speak: The Definitive Compendium of Authoritative Misinformation* (New York: Pantheon Books, 1984), p. 31.

3: What's Holding You Back?

1. *Toward a State of Esteem: The Final Report of the California Task Force to Promote Self-Esteem and Personal and Social Responsibility* (Sacramento: California Department of Education, 1990), p. 4. Copies can be obtained from the Bureau of Publications, P.O. Box 271, Sacramento, CA 95812-0271.

2. Ultimately, there is no such thing as a "negative" or "positive" belief. Beliefs are not good or bad; they are merely interpretations of what we observe. It is possible, however, to judge the consequences of our beliefs. We can say that our behavior or emotions are positive or negative. Thus, although it is not really accurate to label beliefs as positive or negative, we can do so based on the behavior and emotions that result from them. When I refer to negative self-esteem beliefs, that's what I mean.

3. It appears that people who have chronic depression (which manifests as an overwhelming sense of hopelessness and helplessness) and anxiety have been unable to create successful survival strategies. Either they haven't been able to make their survival strategy work—in other words, they are unable to do or achieve that which they said would make them good enough, worthwhile, important, or able to survive—or they've been unable even to create one.

4: How TLM Works

1. If, as occasionally happens, Joan insisted that she did "see" her belief in the world earlier in life, I would point to various objects in the room and ask her where the object is, what color it is, and what shape it is. She would soon realize that anything you can "see" exists in a specific place and has color and size, and so on. Then I would ask, "Where in the room was your belief? What color was it? What shape was it?" Trying to answer these questions is

always sufficient for the client to realize that, although she thought she "saw" her belief earlier in life, she really didn't. In other words, the belief is nothing more than an interpretation of what she actually did see. As I explained in detail in chapter 2 there is no "meaning" in the world. All meaning is interpretation and exists only in our minds, not "out there."

2. An important caveat: Despite all I've just written, I want to warn you against accepting the admonition that "you are responsible for your reality" just because I or anyone else says so. The danger arises from the lack of a distinction between "you" as a creation and "you" as the creator of that creation. You as the creation are not in charge of your life. You are like a robot that must act consistently with its programming (that is, your beliefs). You the creation can't talk yourself out of your beliefs just because you want to. You the creation aren't responsible for most of what you do or what happens to you. On the other hand, when you create—not merely understand or even experience—yourself as the creator you distinguish yourself as the creator of your life. You enter what appears to be a non-ordinary state of consciousness. At that point, you have the power to eliminate beliefs and really are responsible for your reality.

5: Using TLM in Daily Life

1. At present, there are only a few people, in addition to Shelly and I, who have been trained to use TLM to facilitate people when the beliefs are unknown. One of my main priorities is training additional LBP facilitators around the country.

6: Case History Diane: Conquering Bulimia

1. We did the spiritual part of TLM in each session, but I won't repeat it in the following case histories.

2. Other beliefs Diane eliminated during our time together include:

- I'm really not artistically talented.

- I should be able to do things perfectly; if I don't I'm bad.
- Bad people should be punished.
- Overeating is the easiest and most inescapable way to punish myself.
- Sense of life: emptiness, not belonging, separateness, not visible, not heard, void, a black hole.
- Sense of self: not being.
- I have no right to have unless everyone else has.
- I have no right to my husband's money. It's not mine. I should be on my knees thanking him for what he gives me.
- I have no right to ask my husband. It's his hard work and it's his money.
- Marriage is not a shared experience where each naturally shares personal thoughts and possessions with the other.

7: Case History Barry: A Transformed Criminal

1. L. Sechrest and A. Rosenblatt, "Research Methods in Juvenile Delinquency," in H. C. Quay. ed.. Handbook of juvenile Delinquency (New York: John Wiley. 1987), pp. 417-10.

The initial research protocol describes the purpose of the study: "We propose to examine the efficacy of TLM as an intervention to improve self-esteem, to enhance an internal locus of control, and to reduce hostility, social alienation, and antisocial behavior in eight incarcerated criminals. We hypothesize that using TLM to eliminate beliefs such as **I'm not good enough, I'm not worthwhile or deserving, I'll never get what I want, People can't be trusted,** and **I don't matter** will significantly improve self-esteem, enhance an internal locus of control, and reduce hostility, social alienation, and antisocial behavior."

Dr. Sechrest and I decided to administer the Tennessee Self-Concept Scale to all sixteen subjects both before and after the intervention. In addition, subjects in the experimental group would be interviewed at the end of the study to determine the value of the LBP sessions, both emotionally and behaviorally, and their assessment of TLM itself. Shortly after the study was under way, at Dr. Sechrest's suggestion we administered another measure, the Inwald Survey 8 (1S8—A). Moreover, the caseworkers for each of the sixteen subjects were asked to submit a weekly written report regarding the attitudes and behavior of each subject, in addition to filling out a Revised Behavior Problem Checklist both before the intervention and again at its completion. Finally, we agreed to attempt to track all sixteen subjects during the year following the completion of the initial study, although it was unlikely that we would be able to stay in touch with all sixteen after they were released.

    2. Several days after his last session, Barry was interviewed by a local therapist. The interview was videotaped and then transcribed, so that Dr. Sechrest could use what was said as part of the data to be analyzed. At one point, the interviewer said, "Okay. Now, Barry, have there been changes in your feelings as a result of LBP sessions you had with Morty?" A portion of the transcript follows.

B: Yeah, there has. There has been. I feel that the way I used to feel was very negative about things. I feel positive about now, since going through this with Morty. And it has helped me a lot. I feel that a lot of the violence—that the way I used to be very violent—I feel now that that's not necessary in my life anymore.
I: So your feelings of violence have changed.
B: Yeah.
I: Any other feelings that have changed?
B: My feelings toward myself. I used to have very low self-esteem. My self-esteem is high now. I think highly of myself now.
I: Okay. And have you changed your behavior as a result of the sessions you had with Morty.
B: Yes, I have. Like I said, thinking violent, I've changed a lot.
I: Now you're not behaving violent?
B: Yeah, right. There's a few instances where I—you know, before this, I probably would have hurt somebody. But, you know, using my head and thinking—I let it go.
I: Any other behavior changes besides violence?
B: Toward women. I respect them a lot more now. You know.

I: Great. Do you intend to make other changes in your behavior when you get out of here and back to a more normal life?
B: Uhhh. (Pause) Yeah, I do. Plan on, you know, staying positive. Thinking good about things. Not thinking that, you know, worrying about this, and thinking that this could stop me from achieving my goals.
I: Any other changes you intend to happen? Like, you were talking about women before?
B: Yeah, think I'm going to try to—a one-woman relationship, you know? Maybe get married and have a happy family.
I: That's a change. Do you see new possibilities for your life that you did not see before the session started three months ago?
B: Yes. I see myself going to school now. I really had doubts before this. But now I see myself going to school.

     3. Shortly after my last session, officials at Maple Street House told me that the offender who had smoked coke on his weekend furlough had run away. They said he disappeared on the day that results from a random drug test were due, so they assumed he had been using drugs again. Several months later this subject called me on the phone. He wanted me to know that he had not run away because he feared a positive drug test. He had gone to collect some money owed to him, got in a fight, and when the police were called, panicked and ran away. Afraid the police would be waiting for him at the halfway house, he never went back. He told me that despite being broke and looking for work, he never acted on his thoughts of robbing people. He said to me quietly and emphatically, "I'd never do that again." He also commented that even during the fight he was asking himself, "What do I believe that made me so angry that I got in this fight?"
     4.During the thirteen weeks of this study, none of the adult subjects dropped out, although one escaped after his second LBP session. On the other hand, two of the teenage subjects quit after a session or two (and were replaced) and one dropped out after six sessions. During their sessions, the teenage subjects tended to fidget, play with their nails, and look out the window. It was considerably harder to get them to pay attention than adults. One of

the teenagers who completed all thirteen sessions did as well as the adults, and I'd be willing to bet he never again engages in criminal activities—although it is clear that he still has a lot of dysfunctional patterns that could be eliminated. This young man floored me when he said in his exit interview, "I used to think I was mean. I'm not mean. I can be. *I'm* not." There aren't many people who experience and can make a conscious distinction between their behavior and who they are; this fifteen-year-old could. So it appears that TLM can be as effective with teenage criminals as with adult offenders, even though teens are harder to work with and more of them probably would dropout than adults.

8: Case History Frank: Transcending AIDS

1. *Time*, 11 March 1990, p. 76.
2. *Newsweek*, 7 November 1988, p. 88.
3. Bernie Siegel, *Love, Medicine & Miracles*, pp. 4, 88. Here and throughout, facts of publication not given here appear in the Recommended Reading lists that follow the Notes.
4. Ibid., p.3.
5. Jack Gorman, a principal investigator for a National Institute of Mental Health study on the relationship between the course of the AIDS virus and the psyche, says there is evidence that "depression and stress have bad effects on the immune system, while an optimistic and hopeful attitude has good effects." Other researchers claim that the mental state underlying AIDS is that of victim, that is, an external locus of control in which one feels that one is living at the effect of others. The beliefs that were uncovered in my workshops confirm that.
6. I made an appointment with Norman Cousins, the former magazine editor who claimed to have cured himself of a deadly illness using laughter and massive doses of vitamin C. He had joined the faculty of the School of Medicine at UCLA and was very involved in supporting PNI research. Cousins was very open to what I had to say. He even offered to write a letter that I could attach to our research proposal and use for fund-raising. The letter read, in part: "The emerging field of psychoneuroimmunology, or

the biochemistry of the emotions, is turning up significant evidence that the positive emotions have a measurable impact on the immune system and, when this information is integrated with appropriate medical therapies, can produce dramatic results in the treatment of disease. The attached proposal represents an important effort to identify the relationship between psychosocial factors and immune function in HIV-Positive individuals. Results from research of this kind, while focused on the AIDS pattern, may well have an impact on the treatment of a wide range of serious illnesses, including cancer and heart disease."

Dr. Elinor Levy also wrote a letter for fund-raising: "Scientists generally acknowledge that cofactors are important in the development of AIDS, and that these cofactors help explain the fact that one HIV-infected individual develops AIDS within two years, whereas another is still apparently healthy more than ten years later. We believe that psychological factors could act as one of the co-factors for the development of AIDS.

"If this is the case, then clearly any psychological intervention that can ameliorate psychic distress and produce long-lasting effects would be expected to slow the progression of AIDS. The technique developed by Morty Lefkoe, our co-investigator on this project, which is an approach to improve efficacy and self-esteem, could be such an intervention. His intervention also may have broader application in the important area of substance addiction, where low self-esteem tends to be an important factor predisposing to substance abuse."

7. Ken Wilbur, quoted in Larry Dossey, *Beyond Illness* (Boston: Shambhala, 1985), p. 96.

The relevance of this state to illness was captured very well by Dr. Larry Dossey (*Beyond Illness*, p. 61): "Sick people who achieve this awareness (a sense of Oneness, of transcendence) in the course of illness seem to radiate an unmistakable freedom from illness, even though they are afflicted by it and are immersed in it. This is paradoxical, for it is obvious that they are not free from disease: They hurt like other people, they may orient their lives around taking medications on schedule, following certain treatment programs, etc. Where does the freedom they emanate come from?

"It arises because they are not fixated on the fact of illness as if it were an external event that is controlling their lives. Their world, originally a conglomeration of subjects and objects, has undergone the fusion and subsequent disjunction described above as the final state of understanding in which the freeing quality of oneness is retained. It is this unity of opposites that allows freedom from particulars, such as illness and disease. As (Zen writer Toshihiko) Izutsu puts it, 'Man (at this final stage) is a *total* actualization of the Field of Reality, is on the one hand a Cosmic Man comprehending in himself the whole universe. . . and on the other he is this very concrete individual man who exists and lives here and now, as a concentration point of the entire energy of the Field. He is individual and supra-individual.'"

8. Dossey, pp. 146—47.

9. Based on the results of extensive PNI research and the success of TLM in changing attitudes, I still am convinced that TLM can make a significant contribution to health care by improving the functioning of the immune and other systems. I hope to fund either the AIDS study I've described or some other research to determine what role TLM can play both in prevention and treatment of any illness.

9: Raising Empowered Children

1. These are what H. Stephen Glenn calls "adultisms" in his book, *Raising Children for Success*, p. 79.

2. When I conduct individual LBP sessions in a business workshop, I frequently have businesspeople tell me that the most valuable thing they've gotten from the three-day workshop that is designed to change the culture of their organization is a change in their parenting (see chapter 10). Merely watching a few people trace behavior to beliefs and beliefs to interactions with parents in childhood is enough to make most people acutely sensitive to their own behavior and conversations with their children.

3. Some of you might feel "But I am responsible for my children's behavior!" Where did you see that in the world? You never saw in the world that you are responsible for your child's

behavior toward others. That was an interpretation of something you did see. The belief isn't "the truth" it's "a truth." Just take a look at the consequences of operating out of the belief and see if it works for your child—in the long run. Remember this when I discuss other common parenting beliefs that you may be tempted to defend.

4. It is true that there are many ambitious children (and adults) who will not let anything stop them. However, notice two things about that phenomenon. First, the number of people who really feel that they are in control of their lives and can have things turn out the way they want is very small. Second, there are many people who have created a survival strategy that consists of saying **I'm good enough because I won't let anything stop me** or **I'm good enough because of my successes**. (The first was a belief I discovered in myself and eliminated.) Such people frequently succeed by societal standards. But their behavior is compulsive, not chosen freely. The question that should be asked is, "What is the level of their internal satisfaction? What is the emotional and psychological cost of their external success?"

5. According to *Violence and Youth*, a 1993 report of the American Psychological Association Commission on Violence and Youth: "Harsh and continual physical punishment by parents has been implicated in the development of aggressive behavior patterns. Physical punishment may produce obedience in the short term, but continued over time it tends to increase the probability of aggressive and violent behavior during childhood and adulthood, both inside and outside the family. These findings suggest a cycle in the development of aggressive behavior patterns: Abuse at the hands of parents leads children to think and solve problems in ways that later lead to their developing aggressive behavior patterns and to their continuing the cycle of violence."

To those parents who respond, "A few smacks once in a while is not 'harsh and continual physical punishment,'" maybe it isn't to you. But how is it being interpreted by a child, or even an adolescent?

6. Of the twenty-odd recommended readings listed under "Parenting" at the back of the book, the best one I found at this

time was "*Don't Stop Loving Me*" by Ann F. Caron. Later I discovered *Mother Daughter Revolution* by Elizabeth Debold, Marie Wilson, and Idelisse Malav'e, and *Reviving Ophelia*, by Mary Pipher. Shelly and I found both books very helpful in understanding the world as seen by adolescent girls. They also helped us understand that, although parents are the major source of our beliefs, by the time we reach adolescence our culture also plays an important role in determining our beliefs. I also found helpful Haim Ginott's highly regarded book, *Between Parent and Teenager*. Although it was published many years ago, this solid book stands the test of time. The most valuable book of all, in my opinion, is *Positive Discipline for Teenagers*, by Jane Nelsen and Lynn Lott. (I'm probably prejudiced because the recommended behaviors for parents are consistent with my own basic beliefs about parenting.)

10: Organizations That Thrive on Change

1. At Carter Hawley Hale, I developed a three-day workshop that trained groups of the company's trainers. In my first pilot workshops, the trainees reported a number of different beliefs that led to their current situation. For example, one reported that he was quickly promoted on every job he got because his performance was so good, but then something always happened that led to his being out of work: Either the company had to lay off people and he was the last hired and the first fired, or he had a fight with his boss, or he (once) decided to move to a different city. He discovered the belief **I don't deserve to succeed**, which for him totally explained the way his work life was turning out.

Other beliefs that were identified and eliminated by trainees included **I'm not good enough; I'm not worthy; I'm not deserving; No matter what I do it's not enough; Life is difficult;** and **I'll never get what I want**.

None of the trainees had consciously tried to lose his job. In fact, consciously all of them preferred to be working. Thus, initially, everyone thought the idea that their beliefs had anything to do with their employment situation was total nonsense. It was the economy, their lack of education or opportunity, their race, and so on. But, by the time each had done TLM, eliminated a belief, and made real that he created his life, most of them acknowledged that their beliefs had played a major role in explaining the predicament they were in. This is not to say that economic conditions, lack of training, and prejudice have no impact on your ability to get a job. Clearly they do. Nevertheless, the attitudes you project to people, the choices you make, and the opportunities you fail to take advantage of are all a result of your beliefs.

2. Over the years I've collected many evaluations from corporate workshop participants. Here is a sample of what they've told me. You'll see that TLM not only has a positive impact directly on the company, it also transforms the business and personal lives of the people who take the workshops. As you read these comments, ask yourself what type of workforce and work environment would result.

"It helped me to solve my own personal problems so that I can go on to be a more productive person."

"I understand that we live in boxes and that we must change our beliefs before we can change our behaviors."

"You have totally changed my outlook on life, and I plan to make numerous changes at work and at home."

"I now know how to affect behavior, and that means there is no limit to what I can do or what [my company] can do."

"I discovered that I created my life by my observations around me and the way I interpreted the truth as I saw it."

"Understanding why I believe what I believe has allowed me to see things differently."

"I believe that 'real' change is possible."

"It allows me to see how I can fulfill my passion and make my life worthwhile."

In answer to the question, "What was the most valuable part of the workshop?" participants answered:

"To see that I have control over my life and that I create my own life."

"The identification of beliefs as one perception of reality— not as absolute fact! This revelation opened my eyes to my way of viewing the world and its events. I feel more mature and powerful as a result of this understanding."

"Being able to see why the things I want to change or do couldn't be done in the past due to my beliefs."

"Getting rid of the belief that 'I'm not good enough.' This opens many new doors now that I can take risks and it's okay to fail."

"To understand where my feelings were coming from when I was dealing with my child and others I work with. Also, I seem to have more joy in my life."

"The true understanding that beliefs can be changed, because this will allow us to improve both the organization and our personal lives."

"Learning to understand why people do the things they do. And how to use that information to make my job and everyone else's job easier and more effective."

"Finding out why we are what we are. It gives me a different outlook on dealing with people, my family. It gives me a better sense that I can make a difference and that I want to make a difference."

"The part about the possibilities and how our beliefs control our behavior. It opens up new possibilities to reach our corporate mission."

"The realization that it is not someone's fault but a belief they have or the culture that probably is responsible for their behavior. Understanding this means I can focus on the real problem."

"Understanding why people resist change: that resistance is based on their belief system. Knowing that will enable me to deal with resistance to change."

"Realize beliefs control your life, not other people or situations. You can always change. This will make a difference in how/what my future is."

"The one-on-one [LBP] process where I explored a personal belief and discovered it was not 'the truth.' Why—because I truly understand the process [of changing our culture] after I saw my belief disappear."

"Witnessing and realizing that I'm not the only person with the beliefs that I have. They're not bad or good. And most of all that I literally have the power within me to change anything and everything."

"Learning about people's beliefs and how they affect people's behavior. Learning that we can change our beliefs, that we don't have to be limited by our beliefs. The possibilities for what we can do are limitless."

3. Michael Hammer and James Champy. *Reengineering the Corporation: A Manifesto for Business Revolution* (New York: Harper Business, 1993), pp. 60—62.

4. Another way to view the three types of change I describe for organizations is presented in *Steps to an Ecology of Mind* by Gregory Bateson (New York: Ballantine Books, 1972). He distinguishes between three fundamental types of learning: I, II, and III.

Learning I is "a change in specificity of response by correcting errors of choice within a set of alternatives." Using the terminology in this book, Learning I consists of changing your behavior from one option that is consistent with a belief to another option that is consistent with the same belief.

Learning II is "a corrective change in the set of alternatives from which choice is made." Again translating to our terminology, it is a change from one belief to another, which opens up new possibilities of behavior that are consistent with the new belief.

Learning III is "change in the process of Learning II, for example, a corrective change in the system of *sets* of alternatives from which choice is made" (Bateson's emphasis). In other words, it is operating as the creator, not the creation; it is being able to shift "sets of alternatives" or beliefs at will.

Bateson emphasizes that "there might be replacement of premises [i.e., beliefs] at the level of Learning II without the achievement of any Learning III [so] it is therefore necessary to discriminate between mere replacement without Learning III and that facilitation of replacement which would be truly Learning III."

5. William B. Joiner, "Leadership for Organizational Learning," in John D. Adams, ed, *Transforming Leadership* (Alexandria, Va.: Miles River Press, 1986), p. 42.

6. Peter Drucker, *Managing in a Time of Great Change* (New York: E.P. Dutton/Truman Trally Books, 1955), p. 226.

7. Shoshanna Zubouf, *In the Age of the Smart Machine: The Future of Work and Power* (New York: Basic Books, 1988).

8. In recent years many managers who operate out of this belief deny that they hold it because they "know" it's no longer appropriate. The way to determine if a manager has this belief is not to ask the manager, but the workers who report to the manager. Their description of the manager's behavior will allow you to determine quickly what the manager really believes.

9. Some organizations use face-to-face meetings, some use videotapes, some use existing newsletters, and so on. Lands' End created a new publication called *New Directions: Notes from Outside the Box.* The company told all employees that the publication was "a forum written by you, for you. This newsletter will regularly describe the changes that we either have created ourselves or have observed in others. Please keep sending, in a form we can publish, all the changes you are aware of—big and small, first order or second order, in attitude or behavior—that are supporting our new vision and the creation of a third order culture here at Lands' End."

10. The following letter, which was sent by the CEO and vice chairman at Lands' End to 160 executives, managers, and professional staff, captures the essence of what is required to create a Third Order organization.

Dear participants in the two-and-a-half-day Change Workshop:

We have just completed sixteen Change Thinking Workshops which were attended by almost 160 executives and managers. On March 1st we started a series of one-day workshops for most of the rest of the salaried staff, led by Morty, which is a condensed version of the workshop you attended.

We have made this major commitment because we are determined to create a vital, growing learning organization at Lands' End. A company where every one of our employees accepts responsibility for eliminating barriers and creating an environment that supports each person in fulfilling our vision. An organization where everyone is listened to and respected. Where creativity and innovation are nurtured. Where imagination flows. Where mistakes are a part of the learning experience, not something punished. An organization where employees are excited about coming to work.

The evidence is mounting in the business world that employees at all levels—when provided with the appropriate information, training. and support—will accept full responsibility for the success of their company and produce quantum improvements in productivity, quality, and customer service. In fact, as more and more organizations empower their entire workforce, it will be difficult for any organization that does not to survive. . . .

We must shift the role of managers here at Lands' End from figuring out what others should do and then getting them to do it, to creating an environment in which workers figure out themselves what needs to be done to implement the vision, and [are then] empowered to do it themselves.

To create this environment, each of us must accept responsibility for initiating change that supports our daily efforts to fulfill our vision. We must identify the policies, practices, procedures, systems, and structures that inhibit us and then develop alternative ones that will support us.

In the workshops each of you was asked how much of our time is spent actually creating value for customers. You responded that 75% to 90% of your time was wasted overcoming barriers.

We must eliminate these barriers and free up time that doesn't create value for customers. Only by making changes can this be accomplished.

When each of us accepts the responsibility for communicating the changes we have made to the rest of the organization, we encourage others to make changes. We want it to be clear to every single employee that changes are being made, and that everyone is expected to make them. Each manager must prepare the people they manage to take on greater responsibility. (Human Resources has created a number of programs to support you in this endeavor.) When people come to you with suggested changes, remember that we can't say "no." We must be committed to assisting everyone in this company to eliminate the barriers that inhibit them from fulfilling our vision.

Support each other. The changes we must make may not be easy for all of us. We believe that most of us at Lands' End are open to change. If someone responds negatively to your attempt to institute change, don't give up. If we support each other, there's nothing we can't do. . . .

Thank you.
(signed) Bill End and Dave Dyer

11. While I was writing this chapter I called Jim Wessing, the current president of Kondex, and asked if he would send me a letter describing some of the changes in the company that could be attributed to my assistance in helping it create a Third Order organization. Excerpts from his response follow:

People have changed how they look at the world, both here at Kondex and at home. Changing people's beliefs has led to people seeing a lot more possibilities.

Several things have helped facilitate the idea that part of every Kondex associate's job is to make improvements every day here at Kondex. You helped us create an environment in which associates were truly encouraged to make improvements. Part of what helped was creating trust by eliminating punching in and out for the hourly workers and giving every team member the authority to spend up to $100 to make improvements without the need for approval from a manager. This action also supported our efforts to empower Kondex associates to make improvements as they identified them.

In order to communicate the changes that are being made to everyone in the company, we have company-wide meetings every Monday at which we share with each other our goals for the week, what improvements we are making, and any other information of interest to all Kondex associates. These weekly meetings have opened up communication throughout the organization and have allowed a tremendous increase in our improvement efforts.

We had been trying to reduce "cycle time," the number of days it took to run an order through our shop, since 1987. Over the next three years, we had reduced it 58%. During 1991, the year you did your workshops with us, there was a further reduction of 50%. It's now been slightly over two years since you left and we have gotten cycle time down to less than two days. (It is now down to less than 24 hours).

We no longer measure how many reported changes and improvements associates make, but they occur daily here at Kondex. As you know we measured them at one time and we achieved one hundred in a couple of weeks. Now they happen so fast that many of them are shared at our weekly meetings, and many are just implemented without anyone even thinking about them.

I also called Mike Copps, CEO of the Copps Corporation, and asked for a similar letter. Excerpts from his response follow:

Through your leadership we bought into the idea that we're all limited by our personal and corporate belief systems and that if we could remove some or all of these negative aspects of our beliefs we would be much freer with our thought process. Being freer we felt we could arrive at more intelligent conclusions.

The majority of the effort in our group sessions was aimed at eliminating those corporate beliefs that would inhibit us as individuals from doing the job we felt we were capable of doing. Let me add that personal inhibiting beliefs were also dealt with in our group sessions depending on the individual's personal choice. Subsequently each individual took it upon him or herself to change that aspect of the organization that prevented him or her from fulfilling the job.

Once these issues were dealt with, the individuals within the group shared a great sense of freedom to discuss what it is that our organization could and should be. No limitations—no negatives from our corporate culture—no restrictions from the way we used to do things. This allowed us to formulate a corporate mission for our organization. It was our belief that all of the financial variables would fall into place if we were able to achieve our mission. Being in the food business and being a service organization, here is the actual wording of our mission: To create a uniquely satisfying shopping experience in which customers are offered products and services that exceed their expectations.

To accomplish our mission we concluded that there were three absolutes that had to be adhered to. Number one is the mission itself, two is a continual increase in sales and profits, and three is the involvement of all our people. It is noteworthy that there are no other financial variables listed other than sales and profits, and this is purposeful. We don't want our thinking restricted. Any of the other variables such as labor costs, supply costs, advertising expenses, etc. are all trade-offs and not ends in themselves. Our third absolute— involvement—is by far the most important.

Incorporating the above has led us to a method of idea solicitation. We call it our "mission in motion." Anyone in the organization can come up with an idea that represents our mission in motion. We will automatically incorporate that idea. We have developed methods of garnering those ideas from all segments of our business. Our purpose is to accelerate implementation throughout the organization. With our mission in motion we have gone from ideas such as providing umbrellas to our customers on rainy days to wholesale changes in our reporting relationships and responsibilities.

We are continuously working at "getting out of the box." We also discuss regularly going from Second to Third Order Change. There have been enormous improvements in our corporate culture and our ability to communicate with each other as a result of having gone through your process. I might add that our corporate sales and profits have continuously headed upward and that at this moment we are experiencing record profits.

11: Making Society Work

1. Ron Miller, *What Are Schools For? Holistic Education in American Culture* (Brandon, VT: Holistic Education Press, 1991), pp. 153, 156—57.

2. Several books, in addition to Miller's, describe possible strategies, including *The Universal Schoolhouse: Spiritual Awakening Through Education* by James Moffett (San Francisco: Jossey- Bass, 1994); *Schools That Work* by George Wood (New York: E. P. Dutton. 1992); and *New Directions in Education: Selections from Holistic Education Review* (Brandon, VT: Holistic Education Press, 1991).

3. In order to see clearly the power of paradigms in determining an educational institution's purpose, goals, and strategies, compare the mission and strategy of the Mead School, an alternative school in Greenwich, Connecticut, which my two children attended, with the national goals stated in The Goals 2000: Educate America Act.

The Mead School's mission is: "To nurture in each child the power to create a personally meaningful life." Mead expands on this mission by stating:

> The Mead School is a community dedicated to preserving and stimulating the innate curiosity of each child, supporting emotional growth, and encouraging honest responsible relationships. We want students to express personal feelings honestly, and to deal respectfully with the feelings of others. The development of autonomous learning, inner directedness, self-knowledge, responsibility to one's self and the community, and lifelong learning are among our goals.
>
> We value equally the development of a person's mind, body and spirit and in addition to a traditional curriculum—in which art, music, drama and body are vital components—we mean to emphasize concentration, reasoning, investigation, evaluation, decision-making that supports the individual, decision-making that supports the community, intuition, and reflection. Our aim is to encourage students to acquire the skills and confidence to express themselves in all of these conventions.

In contrast, the national education goals declare that by the year 2000, "all students will arrive at school ready to learn; the high school graduation rate will be at least ninety percent; students will be competent in core academic subjects; U.S. students will be first in the world in math and science; all adults will be literate and skilled; every school will be free of drugs and violence; teachers will have a greater opportunity for professional development; and every school will promote partnerships to increase parental involvement in education."

Notice that all these goals are consistent with the current paradigm. Notice also the profound difference in emphasis between Mead's goals and our national goals for public education.

"Goals 2000 is America's blueprint for prosperity and world leadership, and our children's guide to lives filled with productivity and the special rewards that only a quality education can provide."

Notice the emphasis on society ("prosperity," "world leadership," "productivity") rather than on the child/learner, which is consistent with the original purpose of public education, and contrast it with Miller's statements and Mead's focus.

4. The worldview and values that form the basis of our culture and its institutions, especially our science, are primarily the result of the ideas promulgated by two men: René Descartes, a seventeenth-century Frenchman who usually is regarded as the founder of modern philosophy, and Sir Isaac Newton, an Englishman who lived in the same century, who developed the mathematics that validated Descartes's theories.

To Descartes the material universe was nothing but a machine. There was no purpose, life, or spirituality in matter. Nature worked according to mechanical laws, and everything in the material world could be explained in terms of the arrangement and movement of its parts. Descartes gave scientific thought its general framework: The view of nature as a perfect machine, governed by exact mathematical laws. He went so far as to assert, "I do not recognize any difference between the machines made by craftsmen and the various bodies that nature alone composes."

The man who realized the Cartesian dream and completed the Scientific Revolution was Newton, who developed a complete mathematical formulation of the mechanistic view of nature. Newtonian physics provided a consistent mathematical theory of the world that remained the solid foundation of scientific thought well into the twentieth century.

The Newtonian universe was one huge mechanical system, operating according to exact mathematical laws. In the Newtonian view, in the beginning God created the material particles, the forces between them, and the fundamental laws of motion. In this way the whole universe was set in motion, and it has continued to run ever since, like a machine, governed by immutable laws. All that happens has a definite cause and gives rise to a definite effect, and the future of any part of the system could—in principle—be predicted with absolute certainty if its state at any time was known in all details.

The absolute split Descartes made between spirit and matter resulted in a world that could be described objectively, without ever mentioning the human observer. Moreover, this objective description of nature became the ideal of all science. (This summary of Decartes's and Newton's philosophy was taken from *The Turning Point* by Fritjof Capra [New York: Bantam Books, 19831.])

5. Steven Locke and Norman Colligan, *The Healer Within: The New Medicine of Mind and Body*, pp. 8-9.

6. Ibid., p. 10.

7. Thomas Kuhn, in his brilliant book *The Structure of Scientific Revolutions* (Chicago: University of Chicago Press, and ed., 1970), p. 24, points out that most of normal science "seems an attempt to force nature into the preformed and relatively inflexible box that the paradigm supplies. No part of the aim of normal science is to call forth new sorts of phenomena; indeed, *those that will not fit the box are often not seen at all*. Nor do scientists normally aim to invent new theories, and they are often intolerant of those invented by others. Instead, normal-scientific research is directed to the articulation of these phenomena and theories that the paradigm *already supplies*" (emphasis added).

8. Deepak Chopra, *Ageless Body, Timeless Mind: The Quantum Alternative to Growing Old* (New York: Harmony Books, 1993), p.18.

9. Norman Cousins, *Head First: The Biology of Hope* p. 259, 279.

10. In *The Health of Nations: True Causes of Sickness and Well-Being* (New York: Basic Books, 1987), Leonard Sagan has pointed out that those who are competent and have confidence in themselves and in their ability to control their own lives will experience better health outcomes than those who do not... Another dimension that must be incorporated into our notion of health is an understanding and appreciation for the preeminent role of early childhood informing the attitudes and values that are fundamental in the formation of a healthy personality. Our current

biomedical paradigm focuses narrowly on adult behavior, on diet and particularly on physical fitness as the primary determinant of health, and largely ignores the fundamental role of our self-esteem, and our ability to form affectionate relationships with others, and finally, to feel ourselves to be in charge our of own lives. It is in these qualities that true health lies."

Dr. Sagan concludes: "Our health care system should change its emphasis from its current exclusive concern with disease care to also encompass health care. . . . Once we recognize that health is more closely related to pride and self-sufficiency than to trace contaminants in the environment, then the resources and imagination to achieve improved health will become available."

11. Lynda H. Powell, interview, *New York Times*, Connecticut Section, 8 September 1991.

12. An important caveat: There is no firm evidence of which I am aware that any given belief, emotion, or attitude will always cause an illness. The evidence indicates, however, that certain mental states do seem to predispose you to illness; they are cofactors rather than causes. (We all know examples of miserable, depressed, anxious people who were criticizing, complaining, and expressing bitterness well into their eighties and nineties, in seemingly fine health.)

If you have some of the beliefs, attitudes, or emotions that have been associated with specific illnesses (such as heart disease, hypertension, cancer, and immune function disorders), that does not mean you will necessarily get the disease. It is worth noting, however, that the same negative attitudes, beliefs, and emotions that weaken your immune system and predispose you to illness also impair your enjoyment and success in life. When you eliminate them, you not only decrease your susceptibility to disease, you also improve your day-to-day life and experience greater satisfaction.

13. Larry Dossey, *Beyond Illness* (Boston: Shambhala, 1985), p. 8.

14. Despite the fact that the medical establishment and politicians still operate out of the old paradigm, a large number of physicians and an even larger number of patients already have

accepted a new health care model. David Eisenberg of the Harvard Medical School described some startling statistics in a January 28, 1993, article in the *New England Journal of Medicine*. The results of a 1990 survey, Dr. Eisenberg wrote, showed that 34 percent of the American population paid for some form of alternative therapy that year, which included 425 million visits to nonconventional medical practitioners.

Recommended Reading

Parenting

Berends, Polly Bierrien. *Whole Child—Whole Parent.* New York: Harper & Row, 1983. This book incorporates both an in-depth look at the spiritual side of parenting along with thorough chapters on equipment, toys, books, and setting up a nursery. It is divided into ages and stages from prenatal to preschool.

Briggs, Dorothy Corkille. *Your Child's Self-Esteem: The Key to His Life.* Garden City. N.Y.: Doubleday & Co., Dolphin Books, 1970. Self-image is your child's most important characteristic. How to help create strong feelings of self-worth is the central challenge for every parent and teacher. The formula for how is spelled out in this book.

Calderone, Mary S. and James W. Ramey. *Talking with Your Child About Sex: Questions and Answers for Children from Birth to Puberty.* New York: Random House, p. 83. This book is helpful in that it is divided into ages so you only need to read the age-appropriate sections.

Caron, Ann F. *"Don't Stop Loving Me": A Reassuring Guide for Mothers of Adolescents.* New York: Harper Perennial, 1992. Adolescents are different. What works with children up to the ages of eleven or twelve will not necessarily work when the hormones start raging. This book is invaluable for learning what happens at adolescence, what children want and need at that age and how to give it.

Dacey, John S., and Alex J. Packer. *Nurturing Parent: How to Raise Creative, Loving, Responsible Children.* New York: Simon & Schuster, Fireside Books, 1992. A new approach to parenting that shows parents of children from five to adolescence how to foster the formation of positive values and cultivate the personality traits that help children make sound and sensitive decisions.

Debold, Elizabeth, Marie Wilson, and Idelisse Malav'e. *Mother Daughter Revolution.* New York: Bantam Books, 1994. In their introduction, the authors state: "We began to realize that

raising a daughter is an extremely political act in this culture.
Mothers have been placed in a no-win situation with their
daughters: if they teach their daughters simply how to get along in
a world that has been shaped by men and male desires, then they
betray their daughters' potential. But, if they do not, they leave
their daughters adrift in a hostile world without survival strategies.
Being stubborn and/or hopeful and/or naive, we persisted: What if
mothers and daughters were to join as powerful allies in
withstanding the pressures on girls to give up and give in? We
smelled the potential for revolution."

Dreikurs, Rudolf, and Vicki Soltz. *Children: The Challenge.*
New York: E. P. Dutton, 1964. Based on Alfred Adler's work, this
book is considered a classic by many. Although theoretical, it is
simply and thoroughly explained. "People, despite all their
individual differences and abilities, have equal claims to dignity
and respect," is the foundation of Dr. Dreikur's theory.

Dreikurs, Rudolf, and Loren Grey. *A Parent's Guide to
Child Discipline.* New York: Hawthorn Books, 1970.

Edelman, Manan Wright. *The Measure of Our Success.*
Boston: Beacon Press, 1992. We're invited to listen in as a loving
and extraordinarily committed mother gives her children lessons to
live by.

Faber, Adele, and Elaine Mazlish. *How to Talk so Kids Will
Listen & Listen so Kids Will Talk.* New York: Avon Books, 1980.
Applications of the theories of Dr. Haim Ginott. Emphasis is on
communication between parent and child. The techniques offered
are helpful to any interpersonal human relationships. Workbook
exercises are very helpful.

_____. *Liberated Parents, Liberated Children.* New
York: Avon Books, 1974. This book is a result of the authors'
participation in Dr. Haim Ginott's work shops. Highly anecdotal
and a great way to remember how to apply the theories.

_____. *Siblings Without Rivalry.* New York: Avon Books,
1987. A new paradigm for raising siblings. An extremely exciting
book.

Ginott, Haim. *Between Parent and Child.* New York:
Macmillan Co., 1965. Dr. Ginott helps parents remember their

humanness while teaching us how to empower our children. Powerful techniques and tools.

_____. *Between Parent and Teenager*. Macmillan Co., New York: 1969.

Glenn, H. Stephen, with Jane Nelsen. *Raising Children for Success*. Fairoaks, Calif.: Sunrise Press, 1987. Excellent reading for parents of children seven or eight and up. The purpose of this book is to help parents make changes in attitudes and perceptions that can help children find success and happiness. "Parenting can be seen as a chore and a burden or as an adventure with unlimited possibilities."

Kitzinger, Sheila. *The Complete Book of Pregnancy and Childbirth*. New York: Alfred A. Knopf, 1981. The name says it all!

Nelsen, Jane. *Positive Discipline*. Fairoaks, Calif.: Sunrise Press, 1981. Based on the teachings of Adler & Dreikurs, this book gives practical applications of the theories. This is an important book for understanding democratic childrearing.

Nelsen, Jane, and Lynn Lott. *Positive Discipline for Teenagers: Resolving Conflict with Your Teenage Son or Daughter*. Rocklin, Calif.: Prima Publishing, 1991. If you have a teenager and can only read one book, this is it. It is filled with brilliant tools for encouraging self-actualization and building healthy self-esteem. If you are looking for an effective way to raise your teenagers without having to "control" them, this is the book for you.

Pipher, Mary. *Reviving Ophelia*. New York: Ballantine Books, 1994. Many informative case histories that show the impact of the "larger cultural forces" that impact girls today.

Pogrebin, Letty Cottin. *Growing Up Free: Raising Your Kids in the 80's*. New York: Bantam Books, 1980. This book is a powerful example of how raising children with sexism is dangerous to their well-being.

Steinem, Gloria. *Revolution from Within: A Book of Self-Esteem*. Boston: Little, Brown and Co., 1992. Having led a social revolution against sexual and racial barriers of the past two decades, Gloria Steinem now connects that external revolution to a necessary internal revolution of spirit and consciousness. This is her personal journey, along with research and reportage on the meaning of self-esteem in this country and around the world.

Compiled by the Possibilities of Parenting Center, 760 Arlington Circle, Novato, CA 94947. P: 415-884-0552   Fax: 415-506-4263.
e-mail: info@lefkoeinstitute.com.

The Mind-Body Connection

Borysenko, Joan. *Minding the Body, Mending the Mind.* New York: Bantam Books, 1988.

Carlson, Richard, and Benjamin Shield, eds. *Healers on Healing.* Los Angeles: Jeremy P. Tarcher, 1989.

Chopra, Deepak. *Ageless Body, Timeless Mind: The Quantum Alternative to Growing Old.* New York: Harmony Books, 1993.

_____. *Perfect Health: The Complete Mind/Body Guide.* New York: Harmony Books, 1990.

Cousins, Norman. *Head First: The Biology of Hope.* New York: E P. Dunon, 1989.

Dossey, Larry. *Beyond Illness.* Boston: Shambhala Publications, 1985.

_____. *Space, Time, and Medicine.* Boston: Shambhala Publications, 1982.

Harrison, John. *Love Your Disease.* Carson, Calif.: Hay House, 1984.

Hay, Louise L. *You Can Heal Your Life.* Carson, Calif.: Hay House, 1987.

Karasek, Robert, and Tores Theorell. *Healthy Work: Stress, Productivity, and the Reconstruction of Working Life.* New York: Basic Books, 1990,

LeShan, Lawrence. *You Can Fight for Your Life.* New York: M. Evans & Co., 1977.

. Locke, Steven, and Douglas Colligan. *The Healer Within: The New Medicine of Mind and Body.* New York: E.P. Dutton, 1986.

Pearsall, Paul. *Superimmunity Master Your Emotions and Improve Your Health.* New York: Fawcett Gold Medal, 1987.

Pelletier, Kenneth R. *Mind as Healer, Mind as Slayer.* New York: Dell Publishing, Delta Book, 1977.

Roud, Paul C. *Making Miracles: An Exploration into the Dynamics of Self-healing.* New York: Warner Books, 1990.

Sagan, Leonard A. *The Health of Nations: The True Causes of Sickness and Well being.* New York: Basic Books, 1987.

Sarno, John E. *Healing Back Pain: The Mind-Body Connection.* New York: Warner Books, 1991.

Siegel, Bernie S. *Love, Medicine, & Miracles.* New York: Harper & Row, 1986.

Simonton, O. Carl, Stephanie Matthews-Simonton, and James Creighton. *Getting Well Again.* Los Angeles: J.P. Tarcher, 1978.

55063087R00147

Made in the USA
Lexington, KY
08 September 2016

strategy belief like **Being in control makes me powerful**, being out of control brings the self-esteem belief to the surface, along with the anxiety that is associated with it. Verbally and physically abusive behavior with children (and even spouses) is the attempt to get back in control, in order to cover up the anxiety parents feel when they experience being out of control.[5]

Victims Create Victims

A great many adults act as if they believe that someone or something outside themselves has ultimate power over them. They think, "My life would be perfect if only my spouse (or my children, or my co-workers, or my boss) would..." In other words, these people feel they are victims of others. Where does that come from?

In addition to the constant "do this" and "don't do that" that we hear as children, we also frequently hear, "You make me angry [or some other feeling]!" The message is that something outside of us determines what we feel.

Between constantly hearing "no" and "don't" and the message that feelings are a function of something outside of you, it is understandable that people would wonder, "Who am I to determine how my life turns out?" Concluding **I don't matter** or **I'm powerless** is virtually inevitable, given how so many of us were brought up.

Pause for a moment. Is the connection between our parenting styles and the state of society getting clearer? Can you see that virtually all the problems individuals experience—from drug and alcohol abuse, to crime, to relationships that don't work, to people blaming everyone and everything else for their lives not working and experiencing no personal responsibility for changing their circumstances—are the inevitable result of beliefs that were formed in childhood—and those beliefs were the inevitable result of how we were parented and are parenting our children today? You might not like this explanation, but if you are willing to accept responsibility as parents, you have the opportunity to change your parenting. You also have the opportunity to be a part of changing the state of the world.

My Operating Principle as a Parent

At some point I found that I could no longer justify most of my "interventions" as a parent, based on the principle, What is my daughter likely to conclude about herself and life as a result of the interaction I just had with her? Once I had decided that my job as a parent was to enhance self-esteem and sense of life, I created the basic operating belief out of which I parent: **The only time I should forcefully intervene**—that is, tell my children what they must do or cannot do—**is when they are about to do something that will harm them, someone else, or something of value**. Of course, it's not always obvious if harm will follow a given behavior, and it's often a major challenge to figure out how to operate consistently out of this standard. I don't always succeed.

How did I come to create this new operating belief about parenting—in contrast to other beliefs like **My job is to teach my children**? I concluded that experience was a more effective teacher. Think about it: Children learn the two toughest things they will ever learn—to walk and to talk—not from their parents but from direct interaction with reality.

That doesn't mean I can't encourage my children or acknowledge them or give them support and advice; I do this regularly. I offer advice and we talk about the potential consequence of their actions. But when it comes to deciding what they can and can't do, I leave it up to them unless I foresee some harm and can explain my position. Is it harmful for an eleven-year-old girl to have three holes in her ears and stay up after midnight on weekends? (I concluded it wasn't.) Is it appropriate for a thirteen-year-old girl to buzz her hair down to one-eighth of an inch? (I cringed at the thought, but I helped Blake do it after she had carefully considered several questions I raised and still wanted to go ahead. After living with it for a couple of months, she decided to let it grow back.)

I have decided that my opinion doesn't count for more than my children's opinions just because I am their father. If I believe their behavior might be harmful, I will say "no," not just because I have the authority, but because I am responsible for their well-